Copyright © 2016 by Sandra Green

All Rights Reserved.

No part of this book may be reproduced in any form or by any electronic or mechanical means, including information storage and retrieval systems, without permission in writing from the author. The only exception is by a reviewer, who may quote short excerpts in a review.

Disclaimer

Although the author and publisher have made every effort to ensure that the information in this book was correct at press time, the author and publisher do not assume and herby disclaim any liability to any party for any loss, damage, or disruption caused by errors or omissions, whether such errors or omissions result from negligence, accident, or any other cause.

First Edition, June 2016

ISBN 978-1534626546

Table of Contents

		Page Number
Introduction		5
Chapter One:	The Business Imperative	7

PART ONE

Chapter Two:	The Barriers of Organisational Culture	17
Chapter Three:	The Differences in How Men and Women Navigate Their Career	29
Chapter Four:	How Women Hold Themselves Back	39
Chapter Five:	The Age Old Issue of Work Life Balance	47
Chapter Six:	Are You For Real?	55

PART TWO

Chapter Seven:	Suggested Actions for Organisations	63
Chapter Eight:	Setting Your Inner Compass	69
Chapter Nine:	Building Your Inner Confidence	83
Chapter Ten	Becoming a Courageous Leader	91
Chapter Eleven:	True North Leadership	105

Introduction

As an executive coach for women leaders, I noticed over a period of time, a number of recurring themes with women that I didn't notice with men. These themes predominantly focused on issues with confidence and self-esteem as well as issues with getting noticed and respected by colleagues.

Intuitively I felt there were a number of gender specific problems that, despite my best efforts, I couldn't find an easy solution for. It was very difficult to get a clear picture as to what was going on. The more I researched the more confused I felt. There was no 'one-stop shop' to guide me.

I subsequently felt moved and inspired to write a book on the current situation for women in the workplace. I wanted to enlighten both men and women. I also wanted to show the amazing opportunity organisations have when gender diversity is embraced.

There is a tremendous amount of evidence that diversity delivers engaged teams and greater commercial results. There is also, sadly, a dearth of women at the top of our organisations. We must all work together in creating a strong pipeline of talented female leaders.

There was a second reason for me writing this book. And that's for my two children – Zoë and Jack. Zoë is a bright and ambitious teenager. Like her brother, she has bags of potential and wants to make her mark on the world. I know, as hundreds of other women do, that the world of work is not an equal place for women. There is discrimination and there are different rules depending on your gender. I want Zoë to have freedom and equality in promotion, opportunities and career success. And, I want my son to be aware of the issues too, so he can also embrace the female diversity opportunity as he progresses in his career.

According to the World Economic Form, it is going to take 120 years to achieve gender equality. The pace of change is too slow.

As working women, we are the role models to our daughters and to the next generation of women coming through the ranks. We cannot sit back and rest on our laurels. We have to fully understand the reality of what is going on and have clear, practical strategies for doing something about it. This is a business and social imperative.

The book has been split into two halves. The first half of the book focuses on the 36 reasons women don't make it to the boardroom. I was keen to bring together definitions of the language that is used to describe gender inequality, such as 'The Pink Ghetto' and 'The Tiara Syndrome'. The second half is much more practical. It provides a wealth of ideas and resources for what you can do to achieve career fulfilment.

My hope and intention is that this book is a guide and a source of inspiration for you.

Let's get started.

Chapter One: The Business Imperative

Before we look at the reasons for why there are so few women in our boardrooms, we need to understand the bigger picture. Specifically:

1) The benefits that women bring to the boardroom
2) The current picture regarding numbers of women in our boardrooms

The Research Findings

There is considerable research highlighting the benefits of improved performance when women are on boards. Here's a selection of some of the most powerful pieces of research from across the globe:

- McKinsey's Women Matter report found that companies across all sectors with the most women on boards significantly and consistently outperform those with no female representation (41% return on equity and 56% return on operating results).
- Catalyst's Bottom Line report found that companies with the highest percentile of women on their boards outperform those with the lowest as follows:
  o 53% higher return on equity
  o 42% higher return on sales
  o 54% higher return on invested capital
- Once businesses have at least one woman on their board, they have found that the share price of those companies outperform companies with no women by 26% over a 6-year period. (Credit Suisse, "The CS Gender 3000: Women in Senior Management"). In the same report, where there is one female in the boardroom, companies have seen an average return on equity of 14.1% (sector adjusted) since 2005 compared to 11.2% for all male boards.

- In February 2016, Ernst and Young and the Peterson Institute revealed that an organisation with 30% female leaders could add up to 6 percentage points to its net margin.
- Leeds University Business School reports that having at least one female director on the board appears to cut a company's chances of going bust by about 20%.
- A Grant Thornton report found that listed companies in the UK, US and India with at least one woman on their board improved performance over male-only boards by $430bn in 2014.

Global Benefits for Gender Diversity

"Women are the new emerging economy. Women are going to come into the economy, either as workers, entrepreneurs, employees or consumers in such a magnitude over the next decade that it will represent an economic impact third in size behind the economic growth of India and the growth of China." Beth Brooks, Global Vice Chair, Ernst and Young. (2013).

Let's take a look at some more facts.

- According to the Boston Consulting Group (Sept 13), women control 64% of household spending globally. (Women are buying on behalf of others as well as influencing others' buying decisions, such as their partners, children and parents).
- According to an article in Harvard Business Review, "The Female Economy", private wealth in the US is expected to grow from $4trillion to $22 trillion by 2020 - half of this wealth will be in the hands of women.
- The former Chairman and CEO of General Motors (Daniel Akerson) believed that women make 60% of car buying decisions.

- In September 2015, Nike found that "catering for female customers as a growth initiative has contributed to a 15% increase in quarterly revenues."
- There's also considerable research that female leaders bring other qualities to the boardroom, such as building relationships and transformational leadership. The Manchester Research Group (Gender Differences and Leadership) found that women scored higher on getting the job done as well as being transparent and clear.

UK Progress

Back in 2010, the UK Government launched an initiative to investigate the current situation with Women on Boards. At that time there were 12.5% of women directors in the FTSE 100 companies. Lord Davies, who was responsible for the report, set an involuntary target of 25% female representation in the boardroom by 2015.

- Five years on, by November 2015, the FTSE 100 boardrooms have achieved a representation of 26.1%.
- Within the FTSE 250, women currently hold 19.6% of board positions.
- The FTSE 100 no longer has any all male boards.

Many companies are pro-actively doing something about the gender mix. Unilever has doubled the number of women on its board to 50% since 2011; Marks and Spencer has risen from 41.7% to 27.3%; Rolls Royce went from 7.1% to 33.1% and HSBC from 16.7% to 42.1%.

In addition, globally, General Motors, IBM, PepsiCo to name a few, have all recently appointed a female boss.

There have been a couple of other reports looking at the potential growth opportunity for having more women in the workforce:

- If the proportion of women in full time work increased by 5% this would potentially add £700m in extra taxes. (Institute for Public Policy Research)
- The Women and Work Commission report estimates an under-utilisation of women's skills costing the UK economy between 1.3 and 2% of GDP every year.

The Pipeline Issue

- Women comprise 50.3% of the UK's working population age (UK CES Gender Effects (2015). In the same report, researchers found that girls outperform boys at both GCSE and A Levels.
- The proportion of first-degree graduates that are women is 57%.
- The Chartered Institute of Management (2013) in the UK found a 'gender pyramid', i.e. women make up 60% of junior management positions, 40% are middle managers, and 20% are senior managers and single figures for CEOs and executive directors. This is not only a UK phenomenon but also a global one.
- According to the International Labour Organisation (2012), females within the UK make up 34.2% share of all management roles (positioned 19th out of the 49 countries researched).

According to the Human Rights and Equality Commission it will take 70 years to achieve gender-balanced boardrooms in the UK.

The Reality of Boardroom Diversity

Here's the biggest frustration. At the time of writing:

- There are only 5 female CEOs in the FTSE 100 and 2 female Chairs. (That means there are 95 male CEOs and 98 male Chairs).
- Of the 26.1% women on boards only 9.6% are executive directors, i.e. over 30% of women in the boardroom are in non-executive roles.
- Within the FTSE 100, 42 companies still have less than 25% women on boards.
- The FTSE 250 still has 17 all-male boards
- In a New York Times article, apparently there are more men named John running FTSE 100 companies than all female bosses combined.

The Pink Ghetto

The Pink Ghetto describes the plethora of women working in roles such as Communications, PR, HR, Legal, and Corporate Affairs. Take a look in your organisations.
- How many CEOs or Company Presidents are female?
- How many Chief Financial or Chief Operating Officers are women?
- Now take a look around and see how many men are in HR or PR?

Many women either focus too much on their technical expertise rather than getting broader general management experience or they don't get the opportunities to broaden out their skills. Don't get me wrong, this is in not in any way meant to rebuke those women who do a fantastic job in these roles.
It merely demonstrates that getting into an executive position from these directorships is extremely tough – if not impossible.

The Glass Cliff

The Glass Cliff refers to the roles and positions in organisations that are precarious and risky. Two professors from the University of Exeter in the UK first coined the term back in 2004. (Michelle K Ryan and Alex Haslam).

The work by Ryan and Haslam uncovered three interesting facts:
- In law firms, women were given more problematic cases
- In politics they were selected for more difficult to win seats
- Male-led companies only considered the appointment of a woman when they had become financially troubled.

Later research by Susanne Bruckmüller and Nyla Branscombe reported the following:

"When a male run company wanted a new CEO 62% would choose a male candidate – when the company was performing well. However, when the company was not performing as well, 69% would choose a woman!"

Are Quotas the Answer?

Let's tackle the quota debate. For several years there has been much debate about whether quotas are good for an organisation or not. Quotas essentially force organisations to bring in a certain percentage of women within their boardrooms.

Norway, for example, is well known for instigating a 40% quota system several years ago. The UK has introduced a voluntary code (following Lord Davies report 'Women on Boards'). He has suggested that organisations have 30% of positions filled by women by 2020.

Several European countries, including France, Netherlands, Spain and recently Germany are using legislation to create pace and change. If a resolution by the European Parliament (November 2013) is passed, then companies will have to introduce 40% of their non-executive positions for women.

Certainly the many people I've spoken to (both men and women) are absolutely split down the middle, i.e. half strongly believe that we should NOT introduce quotas. The other half believes quotas are a good thing.

There are several reasons so many don't believe or don't want quotas:

- It removes the fairness of being the best person for the job (the meritocracy debate)
- There are not enough women to choose from (lower calibre women may land boardroom roles).
- A lack of general management experience (see Pink Ghetto)
- Coping with the stigma of landing a role because it's perceived as a tick box exercise

Even though these are powerful arguments against introducing quotas, I'm on the side of introducing them. My reasoning? I've been working with many women who sit just below executive board positions. And they are struggling to get through. They are talented, capable and driven women. And, they are frustrated at the lack of recognition and pathways for them to get there.

There are WAY too few women sitting as executive directors in our organisations. Yes, we might not get the best 'woman' for the job. But you can bet your bottom dollar that by forcing organisations to have women in key roles, there will be a rapid and massive focus on sorting out the talent pipeline behind them. With an increased focus we will see more women staying in organisations and, over time, those cultural barriers will disappear.

Without quotas, how else are we going to speed up the process of change and get this on the radar of our organisations?

Part One

Chapter Two: The Barriers of Organisational Culture

Let's take a look at some of the key reasons why women don't make it in the boardroom, by taking the perspective of organisational culture.

Reason 1: Lack of Role Models

Given the lack of women who are sitting in board positions then it's no wonder women find it difficult to access an easy trajectory for their own career. If you only look up and see men at the top of every function, how can we inspire the sorts of numbers we need to get a balance in the boardroom?

In a 2014 survey by the Chartered Institute for Management, "The Power of Role Models", 81% of women said that a role model raised their aspirations. And 55% believed there were NOT enough role models in organisations.

We need real women in real, influential board roles. We need to have talent pipelines that are full of women with real potential and drive to get to the top. With so few women there to guide, mentor and support other women coming through the ranks the pace is going to continue to be painfully slow.

Reason 2: The Glass Ceiling

For women who make it towards the top of their organisations are faced with the well-known barrier of the Glass Ceiling.

In a survey by the Financial Adviser School in 2013, 2000 Britons were asked their views on the glass ceiling. The research found that 89% of women believe there is a glass ceiling that prevents women getting to the top.

I worked with a client, fairly recently, who, quite frankly, was brilliant. Outshone her male peers in every single result and measure she was assessed against. She also won hands down in the engagement stakes too. Guess what. When it came to promotion onto the board, a bloke got the job. Don't tell me that the Glass Ceiling no longer exists. I hear it and see it time and time again.

Reason 3: Gender Stereotyping

Perhaps the biggest issue faced by women at all levels in organisations is that of gender stereotyping.

A study by the ILM (Institute of Leadership and Management) back in 2004, called "Women in Leadership" found that 51% of both men and women found stereotyping to be the major hurdle facing women wishing to get to director level.

Stereotyping refers to a set of assumptions that are believed to be true. Let's look at a few examples:

"Men are different to women, e.g. Men are more competitive, goal oriented and rational. Women on the other hand are more emotional; caring and empathetic."

"Working mothers cannot be as committed as women without children."

"Women do not have the commercial acumen of men."

There's an excellent report by the Fawcett Society looking at gender stereotyping in the workplace. It's called "Just Below the Surface: gender stereotyping, the silent barrier to equality in the modern workplace" and was written by Dr Katherine Rake and Rowena Lewis (2009).

Within the report, there is reference to how women who make it into senior leader positions, have to prove themselves.

"A female leader can expect to be viewed as less competent when her behaviour is consistent with stereotypical 'feminine' behaviour, and as 'un-feminine' when her behaviour is inconsistent with what is expected."

Reason 4: Unconscious Bias

Essentially unconscious bias is a 'natural progra[m] [we all] have. It means that we seek out people who are [similar] – whether that is in looks, in our behaviours, in [values] or in our culture. Having a bias affects the way we beha[ve,] interact with, who gets our attention, who we influence and how we make decisions. The difficulty with unconscious bias is that it is an unconscious process, i.e. we are not aware of this filter on our assessments and decision-making. (Check out the famous Orchestra Experiment, where blind auditions improved women's chances of getting through by 300%!).

It's not just women that are affected by unconscious bias. It may involve age, race, religion, sexuality, etc.

For example, unconscious bias particularly plays out in the recruitment of candidates for a role. It is far less risky to recruit someone 'like us' than to take a risk. With so few women in the boardroom to compare, it's no surprise that men may "unconsciously" choose to select someone like them.

Many companies are now looking to invest in unconscious bias training for employees. In fact Price Waterhouse Coopers, now has unconscious bias training as a mandatory programme for every employee.

This is a big one to tackle as it is not just about gender. Unconscious bias is a natural human process. But it still counts as one very big reason why women don't make it to the boardroom.

Here are two gender specific bias that exist in organisations:

Performance Bias
Women seem to have to work much harder to prove themselves over their male colleagues. There's been plenty of research to back this up. Take a recent Melbourne Business School report, "Gender Equality Project":

*Women are rated as **less task competent** than the men who perform at the same level"* (particularly in male dominated occupations and leadership roles).
- *"Women are seen as having **less potential** and **are less likely to be recommended** for hiring when compared to men"* (with equivalent experience, skills and other job related factors).

Additional research found in Academic Medicine "Interventions that Affect Gender Hiring" identified that:

- "Women who expressed anger" or were "perceived as self promoting" were evaluated negatively.
- Whereas "anger expressed by men" was seen as a strength.

Research at Stanford University's Claymen Institute for Gender Research also found issues with performance review bias. For example, women were given feedback on 'aggressive communication' and 'supportive, collaborative and helpful'.

Men on the other hand were given greater feedback about their technical expertise, confidence and independence. One result was that men were being favoured for leadership positions over women.

Pregnancy & Mothers Returning to Work

The Department for Business Innovation and Skills (BIS) together with the Equal Human Rights Commission (EHRC) completed a report into the topic or pregnancy, maternity leave and women returners in 2015. They found that:

- Almost one in ten mothers said their employer treated them worse when they returned to work than before pregnancy.
- Mothers who felt they were treated worse were more likely to be earning £30,000 a year or more.
- One in 20 mothers said they received a reduction in salary or bonus upon their return to work.

- Around one in ten said they received negative comments from their employer or colleagues as a result of flexible working requests.
- A whopping 17% of women earning £60,000 or more a year felt pressurised to work during maternity or return to work sooner than they wanted.

Reason 5: Leadership Style Differences

Catalyst describes the differences in leadership as follows. The traits that are so welcome in leadership today are as 'Taking Charge' traits (and more often demonstrated by men). Women, on the other hand, are much more like to have 'Taking Care' traits.

In the workplace, women often need to prove themselves against men. So they adopt male traits. These traits include being more assertive and achievement oriented. However, when women display these traits they are often more disliked by others. On the other hand, where women display traits of collaboration, warmth and niceness they are seen as incompetent and lacking authority.

As Catalyst so neatly puts it: '*Too Soft, Too Hard and Never Just Right*'.

There have been hundreds of studies looking into the difference in leadership styles for men and women – dating back to the 1950s. Some early research in the US, back in the 1970s, looked into what made a successful manager. The traits of success were identified as exclusively male. And what are these traits?

- Self confidence
- Competitiveness
- Decisiveness
- Aggressiveness
- Independence

And how do women differ? (According to a 2013 Commonwealth Report: "Gender Differences in Leadership Styles"):

- Women have less preference for competitive environments
- When confronted with uncertainty, women report fear, whereas men report anger
- Women have stronger cultural and emotional intelligence (that's needed for global leadership)
- Women are more risk adverse than men
- Women are better at recognising subtle facial expressions
- Women's leadership style is one that is more people based, role-modelling, clear expectations and rewards

Essential, much of the research finds that women have a greater democratic / participative leadership style. And men? They are more directive and autocratic – taking a stronger command and controlling style.

Another way men and women differ is in something called Transformative Leadership. Often organisations espouse the positive effectives of transformational leadership and there have been found to be gender differences. This style of leadership includes being an inspirational role model; having good human relationships; developing followership and ensuring others have strong motivation.

Women have been found to be much more inclined to a transformational style of leadership rather than a transactional one.

Does Neuroscience Prove It?

There's a further fascinating piece of research done by Dr Ruben Gur. He used MRI technology (magnetic resonance imaging) to examine how men and women think. He found:

"Women have more connections throughout the brain; more connections to memory and better connections to emotional centres." Women are wired differently to men.

One example of this difference is that women often provide more information and detail than necessary. They can be discriminated against for not getting to the point as quickly as men.

Here are further differences in a study by Barbara Annis who co-wrote "Leadership and Sexes, linking Gender Science to Create Success in Business".

- Aggression in men is seen in a positive light, in women it's negative
- Men will jump onto a new challenge and women will ask more questions (and perceived as less confident)
- Men will talk about their accomplishments more than women (and therefore seen as a stronger candidate)

With so many organisational competency frameworks having a strong bias to male / transactional factors, it is no wonder that women are stuck. The drive for greater expediency and decisiveness over collaboration and inclusiveness creates a big problem. Some women decide to adopt these male traits - so they are perceived as being a better fit for more senior leadership positions.

Being a transformational leader is key – but is not clearly recognised or ranked as important by men. Taking on male traits seems to alienate women and create huge waves of dislike amongst their colleagues and teams.

Reason 6: Long Hours in the Boardroom

A study conducted by a Business Roundtable found that on average CEOs worked a 58-hour working week. Many women I coach are working more like a 70-hour week. Leaving home between 6 and 7am and not returning until 8 or 9pm. The demands on the executive are vast and relentless.

The facts are that more men than women are willing to work 58+ hours a week; take work home and do extensive after work professional development. Women have a stronger driver for work and life balance.

Professor Pamela Stone (author of "Opting Out? Why Women Really Quit Careers and Head Home") found that a lot of high achieving women quit because they could not deliver the 60 hours a week their jobs demanded. She found that some women managed to achieve part time work, only to find the 'prized parts of their roles' were given to others. These women therefore began to feel undervalued and vulnerable.

And it's not just a matter of staying in the office. With the growth of international businesses, the demands on executives make their work / life balance ever more difficult. Travelling across the world, with mixed time zones, different weekend patterns mean executives are seeing little down time.

Most executives I know take their blackberries / tablets on their holidays. They cannot face the overwhelming number of emails they know they are going to walk back into. This inability to turn off, for fear of not being on 'top of their game' is real and concerning. If this is the cultural norm, then when women look at the leaders in their organisations – do they really want to be a part of it?

And practically, how exactly is a working mother, especially of younger children expected to be a Mum when her life is rotating around the office. And it's not only working mums that struggle, what about those who have elder care responsibilities?

Fortunately organisations are looking to offer more women flexible working opportunities. Whist this seems to be working well for women at middle management levels it is rare at director and executive level.

Reason 7: Isolation

Linked to long hours is the difficult feeling of isolation. A HBR article back in 2012 looked into the issue of CEO loneliness. The research found that half of CEOs surveyed felt lonely in their role. And 61% of that group believed it was hindering their performance.

As you chalk up more responsibility, the most unfortunate fact is that it gets lonelier and lonelier.

It's odd in a way because as a leader, there are huge demands on your time – endless meetings, phone calls, team requests, peers and stakeholders. Others see you as extremely popular. And whilst you might have a lot 'to do' at work, you may not have many people to bounce ideas around. You are expected to have the knowledge and to be paid to make the decisions. And yet, who is there to support you. Who is there to give you encouragement, be a sounding board, and help you think through tough conversations?

The result is that it becomes lonelier and lonelier. That isolation and loneliness can also create inactivity, a sense of being 'frozen' to make the right decision.
Many women take jobs that are either a serious commute from home or require them to live away from home. A loss of social structures – being away from family and friends; relentless demands at work – causing tiredness; few mentors / advisors or coaches can absolutely take its toll on a leader. Is this what life is all about? Do I really want this for my career? Can I really have a fulfilling career, when I don't have time for anything else?

Reason 8: Stress & Overwhelm

The American Psychological Association conducts an annual survey called "Stress in America". The latest survey (2015) the findings were that more women than men suffered from stress. Women were more likely to *"feel anxious, nervous, overwhelmed or that they could cry"*.

Women want to be appreciated and valued for the work they are doing. A simple thanks, a few words from significant people is often all it takes.

The issue may also be that women will often keep going until they explode or worse, burst into tears. How's that for a brilliant example of 'why women can't take the pressure of significant leadership roles'.

Women are often more likely to internalise their stress. And, in turn, this often leads to health issues such as weight gain, insomnia, migraines, heart palpitations, IBS, loss of libido, aches and pains and overall low energy.

A 2014 Deloitte Study into Human Capital Trends surveyed over 2500 companies in 90 countries. They study described "the overwhelmed employee" (we are referring to executives and senior managers here) with shocking statistics such as:

- People checking their mobile phones 150 times a day
- Employees not able to focus and 'toggling' between screens / tasks every 7 minute
- They also found that 67% of business leaders agreed that employees were overwhelmed.

One of the leading causes of stress amongst leaders is trying to do more with ever reducing amounts of resources. And according to the Centre for Creative Leadership, contributors of stress include managing and motivating people, decision making and working with limited resources. They also found that one of the biggest factors was a competitive peer. Women are more likely to take a back seat when up against a competitive peer, whereas men are happier to compete.

Workplace stress has been with us for some time and does affect both men and women. However, when this is coupled with more women doing their 'second shift' it is no wonder that so many of us feel overwhelmed and stressed.

Summary of Organisational Culture Barriers

- Reason 1: Lack of Role Models
- Reason 2: The Glass Ceiling
- Reason 3: Gender Stereotyping
- Reason 4: Unconscious Bias
- Reason 5: Leadership Style Differences
- Reason 6: Long Hours in the Boardroom
- Reason 7: Isolation
- Reason 8: Stress & Overwhelm

In summary, there are many broader issues within the workplace that hinder a woman's opportunity to progress. These challenges seem to be common to any industry sector – and are felt even more when working in stronger male dominated industries. Organisations have to stand back, re-think and apply new strategies that create a fairer environment for women to succeed.

Chapter Three: The Differences in How Men and Women Navigate Their Career

This chapter focuses on the differences in how men and women navigate their career. There are clear differences in how men manage to get to the top and the way women do it.

Women need to learn more about these tactics and see where and how they are holding themselves back. Whilst some of these approaches seem unfair – this is what happens in organisations. Women need to be much more aware of what really goes on here and make some decisions about their own approaches.

All too often, women decide to keep their heads down and use the same approaches they have done all their life. We'll take a brief look at how schooling may have a strong influence on career strategies.

Reason 9: The Tiara Syndrome

The Tiara Syndrome refers to women who believe that if they continue to work hard, keep their head down and do well....... they will be rewarded by a metaphorical tiara on the head. It's a term coined by Carol Frohlinger and Dr Deborah Kolb. It's also referred to as *'professional modesty'*. Many women believe that if they deliver a fantastic performance, they will be recognised and rewarded with a promotion or high visibility project.

Even more frustratingly, as more women fall under the Tiara spell, more men are getting promoted around them and getting paid more. According to a 2012 study by the American Association of University Women, within one year of graduating, women are already being paid less than men by a staggering 7%.

Education as a Key Influencer of The Tiara Syndrome

Let's take a stroll back in time to how girls respond to the education environment.

Kay and Shipman, the authors of "The Confidence Code", refer to the influence of the playground, the sports-field and the classroom. Many girls get praised for being 'good' and 'working hard' (yes I remember those phrases as though they were yesterday!). Boys seem to get told off a lot more than girls and learn how to deal with it a whole lot better than girls – because they've had to. Consequently, as girls mature they fall into a pattern of hard work, praise and reward. Is it little wonder that so many women continue with this type of conditioning when they hit the glass ceiling?

I was recently speaking with a client who was telling me that she absolutely experiences the Tiara Syndrome. She is so unhappy in her role because she is not getting any recognition for the work she is doing, the results she is getting and the wealth of experience she brings to her job. She finds this so demoralising and is now on course to leave the firm to find an organisation that does value her gifts.

Reason 10: The Ambition Gap

There has been much debate in the media about whether men and women have the same ambition.

A study by the Institute of Leadership and Management ("Ambition and Gender Report", 2010) found that men did indeed have greater ambition than women. The report asked both men and women what their 10-year aspirations had been. In terms of achieving a director level 20% of men had this ambition v. 14% of women.

A study by McKinsey and Company in 2014 ("Moving Mind-Sets on Gender Diversity"), reviewed almost 1500 global executives. The research found that the same percentage of men as women strove to achieve top management (approximately 82%). Yet female executives were much less certain they would reach the top (69% women v 83% men).

More recently, a study conducted by Bain and Company ("Companies Drain Women's Ambition After Only Two Years",

May 2015), found that when women join an organisation 43% have an aspiration to achieve top management. After 2 years this drops to 16%.

Perhaps the issue then is not with women who are near to the glass ceiling, but those women earlier in their careers who give up and opt out.

The women I work with are typically juggling many different roles in their lives. Whilst some may have an inner desire and ambition to climb to the top – they hold themselves back by the perceived issues of holding down such a big role.

A similar report to a Wharton University article (Generation and Gender 2004), more women business leaders than men 34% v. 21% have scaled back their career ambitions.

Reason 11: Differences in Job Application

There are some interesting anecdotes about the differences in the ways men and women apply for jobs. Sheryl Sandberg cites, in her book "Lean-In", an internal study carried out by Hewlett Packard (HP). In the study HP investigated why fewer women than men applied for senior posts. One of their findings was that women were considerably less likely to apply for a job if they could not 'tick' every box in the job application experience form.

The Institute of Leadership and Management in the UK studied 3000 managers (2011). They found that 85% of women would only apply for a job if they met all or most criteria for the job. When I recite this tale to other women, I get a lot of nods and echoes of agreement.

The European Institute of Leadership and Management also found the following:

'20% of men would apply for a role despite only partially meeting its job description v. 14% of women.'

Another research study based on four UK universities (Doherty and Manfredi 2005) shows that in the opinion of senior academic staff women are more reticent to put themselves forward for promotion and more likely to undervalue their achievements.

Researchers from Yale University asked 127 scientists to review a job application of identically qualified men and women. They found that all scientists (whether men or women) consistently scored higher for men and were more likely to hire the men. There's that unconscious bias playing out again.

Here's another interesting perspective. The language in advertisements is also a 'turn off' for women. Further research by Technische Universität München (TUM) found that women were less likely to apply for positions that used words such as: "Assertive"; "Analytical"; "Independent". Instead women were more likely to apply for positions with words such as "Dedicated"; "Responsible"; "Sociable". And yet wording on the advertisements made no difference to men.

Reason 12: Negotiation

In an excellent Harvard Business Review article, back in 2003, entitled "Nice Girls Don't Ask", there were a number of interesting facts shared. Here's one that stood out for me:

Only 7% of women negotiated their initial salary when offered a job. Compare this to 56% of men negotiating their first salary.

Interestingly, over the past decade a male graduate could expect to earn 20% more, on average, than a female graduate.

Linda Babcock author of "Why Women Don't Ask" found that men with MBAs earn more than women with MBAs despite doing the same / similar job.

In an experiment at the University of Texas, women were able to ask for the same rate of pay as men – when doing so on behalf of someone else!

Another reason is that women tend to have lower expectations than men. Research by McGinn and Bowles *("When does Gender Matter in Negotiations", 2005)* found that women have lower expectations than men when negotiating. When women decide to negotiate a package, they don't demand as much as men would. Women don't put the same emphasis on their qualities, their skills and their experience. In other words the value they are bringing to the role.

Women are notoriously bad at not recognising their value. This is something I work so hard at when coaching women – giving them the confidence to know what their strengths and uniqueness is. Once we have that, it makes it much easier to know our worth and therefore to negotiate harder.

Another concern is that women don't plan or prepare as well as men. They tend to accept on face value what is presented as a salary / rise with a sigh of relief – *thank goodness that's over with.* Yet women would always plan and prepare so much more thoroughly in every other work situation!

In Sheryl Sandberg's popular TED talk she describes the differences in the way men and women attribute success. For men a typical response may be: "I'm awesome". For a woman, she is more likely to respond, "I was lucky" or "I worked hard". How can a woman ask for more when she is likely to show her confidence in her abilities?

Reason 13: Networking

There's been plenty of research into the differences in how men and women network. One of the best studies has come from Toulouse School of Economics in France in 2011. They found that a major factor in why female directors earn 17% less than their male counter parts was because they were *"less good at building networks"*.

Women typically want to build relationships. They come to networking with a view of how can I help you? Let me get to know you, find out more about you, see how we may be able to help each other in the long term.

Women like to create connections and because women are so good at listening we like to focus on the other person. Women value authenticity.

Men on the other hand, think – who has what I want or need right now? It's a much more transactional approach. There's no hard feelings or a need to get to know others.

A Harvard Business Review Blog by Athena Vongalis-Macrow investigated the ways in which women network. They found that only 4% of women would talk about their career aspirations and goals for fear of appearing too ambitious and risking failure.

Is networking important?
According to research by BNI (Business Networking International) a staggering 50% of jobs are secured through referrals.

Unfortunately one of the differences in men and women networking is that men will create a network that's predominately men. A woman's network will be a blend of men and women. And why does that matter? Well, when the informal networks hot up – news of promotions, new postings, high visibility projects, and international assignments – men will spread the word quickly to their male counterparts. Typically women don't get to hear of these opportunities or hear about them much later than men.

I also love this quote by Sheila Wellington (previous President of Catalyst):

"Men head for drinks, women head for the dry cleaners".

Reason 14: Visibility

Visibility is all about being seen in the workplace. As the old phrase goes: 'Out of sight, out of mind'. Yet women unfortunately are not good at pushing themselves in the workplace. One of the issues referred to earlier was that of The Tiara Syndrome – where women keen their heads down and wait to be recognised.

Catalyst, the US based research body into the advancement of women, released a report back in November 2012. It's entitled "Good Intentions, Imperfect Execution? Women Get Fewer of the Hot Jobs Needed to Advance". What a fantastic title for a report!

Let me share some of the headlines of this study:
- International assignments predict advancement. More men than women land these assignments – 35% v 26%. More women than men were *never* offered them – 64% v 55%.
- Men lead projects that were twice the size of women; had three times as many staff; posed a higher risk to the company and had more C-suite visibility.
- More men were promoted within a year of completing a formal leadership development programme than women (51% of men v. 37% of women).

How shocking are these findings? And whilst the opportunities may be given more to men than women, there are fewer women who want to put themselves forward for these positions as well. Women have less confidence and dislike having to talk about themselves and their achievements.

Yet without the ability to share your performance and achievements true success will always be out of reach. In addition, women need to put themselves forward for stretching roles (yes even without being able to tick all of the boxes) and prove that they can do the leadership and business critical tasks.

A study by GE found that three factors affected people's perception of potential: your performance, your image and your level of exposure. Where do you put most of your efforts? For most women it's on their performance.

Reason 15: Mentoring

Let's start with some statistics as to why mentoring is so important. Sun Microsystems compared the career progress of approximately 1,000 employees over a 5-year period and here's what they found:

- Employees who received mentoring were promoted FIVE times more often than people who didn't have mentors.
- Mentors were SIX times more likely to have been promoted to a bigger job

What's great about mentoring is that it's a two way street. The mentor often gains as much as the mentee, such as: developing their own skills (listening, questioning) and gaining insights into different parts of the organisation.

If mentoring is so effective in managing successful career, what exactly is going on?

One piece of research (Levo League and LinkedIn 2011) found that 95% of all women had never sought a mentor at work. This is staggering.

And for senior leaders 1 in 5 women had never had a mentor.

Often the mentors that women select are not at the same level as the mentors' males select. (There's also some interesting research into the lack of suitable role models – which we will come onto).

There are also differences in what men and women offer when they are mentoring. For example, male mentors are more likely to provide specific help around career issues. Female mentors are more likely to provide help with shifting limiting beliefs, confidence issues and building self-esteem.

Mentoring also helps men more than women in terms of landing 'upper-level' positions. Catalyst completed another report into "Mentoring - Necessary But Insufficient For Advancement". Here's what their research found:

- Men who had a mentor were 93% more likely to be placed at a mid-manager level or above than those men without a mentor
- Women with an mentor increase their placement by 56% over those women without a mentor
- More men than women had a mentor at CEO level

There is of course, the issue of the pool to select from. There are so many more men operating at board level than women. More women want to have a female mentor – someone who has been there, experienced the challenges and risen through the issues. More men want to secure a male mentor.

So, it's clear that women do need to get mentors to help. What we also know from the research is that men will achieve more from getting a mentor than women.

Reason 16: Sponsorship

In 2008, the Equalities and Human Rights commission wrote a powerful report, "*Sex and Power*". Their findings highlighted that at the current rate of change it will take more than 70 years to achieve gender balance in the boardrooms (for the UKs largest 100 Companies).

An earlier report by Derek Higgs and Laura Tyson *("The Recruitment and Development of Non Executive Directors"*, London Business School, 2003) highlighted some fascinating findings:

- Half of the directors they surveyed had been recruited through personal friends and contacts
- Only 4% had a formal interview
- 1% obtained the role through an advertisement.

Recently I interviewed many successful women leaders of organisations. It was no surprise to me to hear that they put their successes down to the involvement of one or more sponsors.

Reading "The Sponsor Effect: Breaking Through the Last Glass Ceiling" (Harvard Business Review Research Report, December 2010) I was shocked to read the following:

While men in general are 25 percent more likely than women to have a sponsor, senior level men are 50 percent more likely to have one.

Summary of the Differences in the Ways Men and Women Navigate Their Career

- Reason 9: The Tiara Syndrome
- Reason 10: The Ambition Gap
- Reason 11: Differences in Job Application
- Reason 12: Negotiation
- Reason 13: Networking
- Reason 14: Visibility
- Reason 15: Mentoring
- Reason 16: Sponsorship

As this chapter highlights, men and women navigate their career journeys differently. We know that the percentage of men over women is much higher at the top of our organisations. We have to teach women the tactics men use and we have to guide organisations to change their approach when recruiting, promoting and development the female pipeline.

Chapter Four: How Women Hold Themselves Back

One of the biggest criticisms I hear is that women are not visible and hold themselves back. There's another terrific book by Sheryl Sandberg (COO of Facebook) with the title "Lean In". This chapter looks at all of the reasons I believe women don't lean in and how they are holding themselves back. How many do you recognise?

Reason 17: Lack of Presence

In a recent survey sponsored by Marie Claire, American Express and Goldman Sachs, one of the key insights was that women who want to get on struggle because they have a lack executive presence. Put more simply, women don't act or look the part.
Research by Sylvia Hewlett founder of the Centre for Talent Innovation states that executive presence accounts for as much as 26 percent of a woman's success in her career.

There are many words used to describe executive presence: gravitas; authenticity; impact; authority.

We can use these words to explain presence, but it is much more difficult to make this come alive.

I remember coaching a high profile leader who wanted a place in the boardroom. The CEO said that she had to improve her presence. When we asked what he meant by that – he said, "You know, presence". Well, that didn't help a great deal! He followed up with *"Others noticing you in a room and remembering you"*.

And I think that's a great way to think about presence. Who is remembering you and what are they remembering you for? What happens when you walk into a room? Do others sit up and take note or have they barely realised you are there? When you speak to the room, are others taking notes, challenging you, supporting you or ignoring you? Do you allow your peers to take the air space?

Reason 18: Lack of Confidence

Confidence and self esteem is something that many working women struggle with. As defined in the book "The Charisma Myth":

Self-confidence is our belief in our ability to do something and / or our belief in our ability to learn how to do something

Self-esteem is how much we approve of or value ourselves.

A survey by the Institute of Leadership and Management ("Ambition and Gender" 2011) revealed the following:

- 70% of men have high levels of confidence compared to 50% of women
- Half of women managers admit to feelings of self-doubt, but only 31% of men do
- Women with low confidence have lower expectations of reaching a leadership and management role and are actually less likely to achieve their career ambitions

And Columbia Business School found that men tend to over-estimate their strengths by 30%.

Now that's a depressing picture!

Reason 19: Our Beliefs and Conditioning

I recently re-read the brilliant Book "The Big Leap" by Gaye Hendrix. In the book he shares his story of how he held himself back from ultimate fulfilment and success due to something he's labelled 'the Upper Limit Problem'. He describes in detail how our beliefs hold us back. A belief is typically a meaning that we give to an event or series of events that we experience.

One of the ways to change our experience of life is to examine and change our beliefs. Firstly we must identify those beliefs that are holding us back and are sitting in our subconscious.

Here are three common belief patterns:

- *I'm not good enough / I want to be accepted*

This belief pattern stops women from taking big leaps in her career, whether that's asking for more money, going for a promotion or stepping up to a big visibility project.
A number of years ago (2006) the Priory Group published research from 1000 women entitled "I'm Not Good Enough". Their research found that millions of women suffered from low self-esteem.

- *I'll get found out.*

This is otherwise known as the Imposter Syndrome. Dr Pauline Clance and Suzanne Imes coined the term in 1978. They defined it as *"....high performing individuals marked by an inability to internalise their accomplishments and have a persistent fear of being exposed as 'fraud'."* The result of this thinking is that it drives women to do several different things. Sound familiar?

- *I fear success*

This term first originated from Matina Horner back in 1968 to explain why women were not achieving their full potential. Firstly, this fear of success belief is not that women are afraid of achieving a particular career goal. Instead it is the fear of consequences of that achievement.

For example, the inner tape playing over and over: What impact will this have on my health and well-being? Can I withstand the stress that this may cause? Is it worth the effort, the long hours, the battles?

External factors typically rotate about the big fear of other's reactions. How will my husband / partner react if I am more successful? What impact will this have on my children? How will other men in my life – father, brother, and other male influences react? Will I be faced with cynicism or jealousy? What about my friends? Can I cope with being the one that's different?

Reason 20: Language Patterns

The author of "How to Say it for Women", Phyllis Mindell believes that women hold themselves back simply by the language they use. How many of these do you fall into the trap of using?

Excessive Use of the 'I' word

- *"I'm not getting on with my boss. He seems to value other members of the team."* Or
- *"I'm overwhelmed and I just can't finish that job."*

Can you see how these statements lack power and impact?

By overusing the word 'I' suggests that you are the cause of the problem or that you have to solve the problem or perhaps the problem is too big to be solved by you. Secondly, the impact is that you are not sure of your facts.

Instead we need to cut out the word 'I'. Here are a couple of alternatives:

"My boss values the efforts of other people in the team" or *"More time / resources would help us get that job finished"*. These are much more impactful than our first attempts.

Using Hedging Language

Again women prefer to 'soften' the impact of their words. Here's how we often lose our power:
"Well...."
"I think......"
"Basically...."
"I guess....."
"I just......"
"I might not be right but......"
"Should....."
"So....."

Whilst men and women use hedging language, according to Phyllis Mindell, women use them much more!

Raising Your Voice at the End of a Sentence

Have you ever made a statement and then softened it by raising your voice at the end?
Often the rationale is to see what level of buy in or engagement we have. Secondly, it's because we are concerned about coming across as too aggressive – instead this makes us much more passive.

Modifiers

Probably one of my favourites and, yes, I absolutely still fall into the trap of using modifiers... Modifiers fill pauses and aim to add impact to our statements*:*

"Really" or *"that's a really good idea"*
"Very" or *"that's a very, very important suggestion"*
"Careful" or *"I was so careful when I was putting the budget together"* or one of the most common phrases around *"Be careful"* (note that one if you have children).

Reason 21: Being a People Pleaser

In our hearts, the majority of us want to please others. It is a natural human drive to please people we are close to and have meaning for us. People pleasers want to meet others needs, to agree with others, to fit in and at times become what others want us to be.

And, we are certainly not flawed in any way by having this innate desire to please other people.

Yet, what we do need to be mindful of is when this desire becomes our overwhelming driver in life. Just think for a moment about the opposite of pleasing people. Displeasing people. So when we have this driver, we are fixated on doing all that we can to *avoid* displeasing others.

How does this play out?

Okay, so if we are motivated more by pleasing others and putting them first, here's what might happen at work:

- Conflict avoidance (not confronting challenges quickly or at all)
- Frustration from others around us (perceived lack of decisiveness and lack of boundaries)
- Over collaboration (and not getting anything done with speed)
- Lack of risk taking (I need to ensure everyone is happy first)
- Hesitation in leveraging relationships (worry about taking advantage of others)

From an external perspective the 'addiction to approval' consequently leads to poor leadership. There's a great quote by Lois Frankel:

"Women are so good at building effective relationships that we often confuse leadership responsibilities with a desire to maintain those relationships at all costs."

What about internally?

Well, typically people pleasers experience several (unhelpful) inner tapes running in their minds. Let's take a look at some of the common ones:

- *People will love and accept me if I do what they want*
- *I can't say no to him, her, them*
- *Whatever will they think?*
- *I want to get along with everyone*
- *Why doesn't he / she return my call?*
- *I'm afraid to speak my mind*

- *I don't want to rock the boat*
- *I'm not sure what it is that I want*
- *I don't want to put my head above the parapet*

The people pleaser syndrome lies at the root of many stress-related problems. Be warned you will find it very difficult to take a leadership role that demands decisiveness, vision and direction if your over-riding desire is to please others.

Reason 22: Perfectionism Thinking

Through my coaching work and in my own personal experience I've recognised a lot of women seem to struggle with 'perfectionist thinking'.

Before we become too critical, it is worth noting that the inner drive to perfect and better you is a very powerful force. Take Olympic athletes and sports starts. Their inner drive to be better and better can lead to extraordinary achievement and success.
It's all about balance.

Gordon L Flett a psychologist professor at York University Toronto stated *"more than 50% of today's Western School aged children exhibit perfectionist traits"*. And *"most high achiever women suffer from some form of perfectionist thinking"*. So, you are not on your own!

And another piece of research by Dr Robert Hurley and James Ryman of Fordham University found *that 30 – 35% of executives under-performed because of perfectionist thinking*. ("Making the Transition from Micromanager to Leader").

Summary of the Ways Women Hold Themselves Back

- Reason 17: Lack of Presence
- Reason 18: Lack of Confidence
- Reason 19: Our Beliefs and Conditioning
- Reason 20: Language Patterns
- Reason 21: Being a People Pleaser
- Reason 22: Perfectionism Thinking

As we've shown in this chapter, it's not only that organisations are inflexible or have out-dated attitudes. Women must learn to help themselves.

All of us can work on 'Leaning In' more as Sheryl Sandberg once put it. We must recognise that our lack of confidence manifests itself in so many ways. And the great news is that we can build strong inner and outer confidence. There are many tricks of the trade that I'm going to share with you!

Chapter Five: The Age Old Issue of Work Life Balance

It is interesting how women are the ones with this at the forefront of their mind. One of the first questions we ask successful women is "How do you juggle it all?". Yet this is not something we ever ask a successful man. There is a tremendous amount of societal conditioning together with the working mothers guilt that us mums experience.

Back in 2012, Anne Marie Slaughter headlined "Why Women Can't Have it All". She described how she stepped down from a high profile government position in America to spend more time with her teenage children. She talked about how she once espoused the belief that women could have it all. And then realised that it was very difficult for women to achieve this.

This is backed up with research by PEW ("A Gender Reversal on Career Roles"). Researchers found 66 percent of women rate career as a high priority and 56 percent of working mothers saying how difficult it is to balance a career with a family.

Reason 23: Opting Out

Lisa Belkin, first coined the phrase 'opting out' in 2003 to describe "highly educated, high achieving women who choose to put aside their careers". (See New York Times Article: "The Opt Out Revolution").

Why do women opt out?

Some women are choosing to opt out because of the lack of flexible working. In 2009, the Centre for Work-Life Policy survey of 'highly qualified' women found that 69% would not have done so if their workplace had offered greater flexible working.
Referring back to the early Harvard Business School survey (see "Rethink What you know about High Achieving Women"), the

findings were that for those women who chose to 'opt out' did so "reluctantly and as a last resort". Why? Because they experienced stigmatism for changing work hours, not given opportunities or losing out on previous high profile projects.

Interestingly, women who choose to change career (over 70%) move into teaching, fund-raising and counselling roles.

Reason 24: Off Rampers

'Off-Rampers' describes talented and highly educated women who voluntarily leave their jobs for extended time periods. Reasons including child-care, eldercare, burnout and overall dissatisfaction.

Two surveys have been completed one in 2004 and the other in 2009. (This was a task force of organisations including Ernst and Young, Goldman Sachs and others). The survey found that 37% of women off-ramped for an average period of 2.2 years. Whilst childcare was the predominant reason for off-rampers other reasons from these surveys revealed:

- 24% felt it was due to eldercare
- 24% stated it was due to un-satisfying jobs
- 23% felt stalled in their career
- 6% was due to the workload being too demanding.

In 2010 the Centre for Work-Life Policy found that 90% of women who off-ramp want to on-ramp back into the workforce. And here's what happened to those women:
- 73% of women who off ramped had trouble finding a job
- Those that did return lost 16% of their earning power
- Of those that returned, 25% had a decrease in their management responsibilities and 22% had to step down to a lower job title
- Only 40% were able to successfully return to full-time work

Interestingly, A 2014 survey by London Business school to over 2000 women found that 70% felt anxious about taking a career break whether that's for children or for travel.

Reason 25: The Mommy Track

There seems to be mixed reviews on the impact having children have on a woman's career. The 30 percent club, recently produced an article: "Cracking the Code". The researched (based upon the UK's FTSE 100 & 250 companies) 'debunk the myths' of women about progression in the workplace.

"While childrearing does slow down a woman's career progression, the research did not find a significant impact on their overall ability to get to the top."

Compare this to research in the excellent book "Do Babies Matter: Gender and Family in the Ivory Tower". This research looks specifically at academia and finds that an astonishing 132 percent of working mothers end up in lower paid positions.

This is backed up by another research paper: "Getting a Job: Is there is a motherhood penalty" published in the Chicago Journal, which found that working mothers were perceived to be less competent and committed compared to those women without children and therefore less likely to be hired. Those that were hired had a 7% lower starting salary than non-mothers and were considered less likely to be promoted.

In an interesting study by Harvard Business Review (over 25,000 HBS graduates) 77% of respondents (73% of men and 85% of women) reported that "prioritising family over work" was the NUMBER ONE barrier to women's advancement to work.

Further investigation into the impact of having children was conducted by economists from Harvard and Chicago universities (The MBA Mommy track). They found that in a study of MBA graduates, men earn 70% more than women nine years later.

Reason 26: Motherhood Guilt

Many working Mums feel desperately guilty that they are not spending enough quality time with their children. A study by NUK in early 2013, found that mothers feel guilty in a variety of ways:

- Missing important events in children's lives such as school plays, sports days, parents evenings, recitals, etc.
- Not giving their children things they want or having enough days out as a family
- Some mums felt guilty for putting their children in front of the TV
- Relying on childcare / nurseries to look after children also added to the guilt
- Being too busy to give their children attention

And as our children grow older there's other form parenting issues that can drive such a lot of guilt:
- Getting into trouble at school (*if I'd been around more this wouldn't have happened*)
- Taking drugs (*they always swore they never would, what did I do to make them do this*)

In another report by child psychologist Dr Claire Hasley who surveyed 2000 parents of children aged 3 to 18, *42% of working parents felt they were not a good enough parent during the week*. And 25% felt they did not have the time to reconnect with their kids in the evening.

It does feel a bit of a double edged sword – feeling guilty being at work when we have left our children at home and then feeling we are not contributing to our best at work, because we have a family. This is not helped by the enormous expectations we place on ourselves.

As working mothers we must take comfort from Professor Heather Josi's research:

"Women going out to work has, in fact, ZERO effect on children's cognitive and literacy scores or on their emotions and behaviour."

And how about this insight: Employed mothers in 2000 spent as much time interacting with their children as mothers without a job in 1975! (Bianci et al., 2000).

Reason 27: Eldercare

Eldercare is essentially providing help to aging parents and relatives. This can be practical help such as grocery shopping; medical visits; helping with paying bills and other administration. Whilst this help is essential, there is also considerable emotional help that is needed. This is much more difficult to measure and is often something the carer has to burden. Seeing a parent with any disease is distressing and having to juggle demands of a career, the practical help required plus the emotional roller coaster can of course create considerable stress.
Here are some powerful statistics:

- According to the Institute of Public Policy Research (IPPR) "by 2017, the number of older people needing care will outstrip the number of adult offspring that are able to provide it". And by 2032, 1.1 million older people in England will need care from their families (an increase of 60%). ("The generation strain: collective solutions to care in an ageing society").
- Carers UK have found that workers in the 45-64-age range are most likely to be looking after elderly parents.
- My Family Care's 2011 study found that 60% of women had eldercare responsibilities.

In January 2010, my father passed away from CJD. This was a terrible shock to me as my father was 68 and had been a very fit and positive man. To see his body waste away in a matter of 2-3 months was very distressing. Supporting him, being there for him whilst running a business was tough. For women who have to care for elder relatives over a much longer period of time, this must find this incredibly hard thing to do.

In a MetLife survey (1999), 16% of respondents said they had to give up their jobs in order to care for elders, a further 64% called in sick or used holidays.

Some of the worst effects of the growing eldercare problem is burnout, depression and of course reduced performance; leaving early / arriving late and absenteeism issues for organisations. So this is a very real and growing problem that absolutely affects how many women can reach the boardroom (and make a full contribution once they are there).

Reason 28: Second Shift

Second shift refers to how looking after the home and in particular children has to be managed outside of working hours. These include cooking, laundry, cleaning, child-care, shopping, admin, health appointments, planning holidays, events, etc., etc.
And the research found that despite working full time – *the majority of women still do the household chores.*

One Harvard review asked men and women about who would be responsible for childcare and 75% of men said it would be their wives.

Research by BBC Radio 4's Women's Hour in 2014 found that whilst men are helping out more around the home, the majority of tasks still fall to the woman. They found that women spend on average 11.5 hours on housework compared to 6 hours by men.

And the reason that a Second Shift is an issue? Most women who do the burden of the second shift are plainly just too knackered to climb that greasy poll.

Reason 29: Part Time Work

Part time work started to grow in the 1960s and during the 1970s half of all employed women were working part time. During the early 1980s, two thirds of the jobs women took on returning to work after childbirth were also part-time.

One seemingly straightforward solution for women leaders who have children is to work more flexibly. And yet the reality for a lot of women is that part time work is stifling, boring and lacks the opportunity for stretch and growth.

In 2005, The Equal Opportunities Commission produced a fascinating report called: "The Hidden Brain Drain". The term means that too many skills are trapped in low-skilled unfulfilling roles. The report investigated flexible and part time working:

- The report found that 5.6 million part time workers (four out of five) are working in jobs that do not use their full potential.
- Two million of them believed they could "easily work at a higher level"
- Part time female workers earn 40% less per hour than men working full time (about the same as the pay gap 30 years ago)

Further research by Dr Sara Connolly from Norwich Business School found that the longer the spell of part time work, the less likely women were to move back into full time – often never recovering their previous career trajectory.

Summary of Work Life Balance Issues

- Reason 23: Opting Out
- Reason 24: Off Rampers
- Reason 25: The Mommy Track
- Reason 26: Motherhood Guilt
- Reason 27: Eldercare
- Reason 28: Second Shift
- Reason 29: Part Time Work

As mentioned at the start of this chapter, achieving work and life balance is one tricky thing to pull off. We are torn between the inspiration we often feel for our careers and the difference we can make and our desires to be excellent mothers.

Organisations can certainly help with removing bias, providing greater flexibility and allowing parenthood to be talked about by both men and women.

Faced with such difficulties in juggling our homes with our careers; issues around societal conditioning and working mother's guilt, is it no surprise that we are faced with such a shortage of women in the boardroom?

Chapter Six: Are You For Real?

A look at some of the more bizarre things that go on in organisations that may well be at the heart of why women don't progress to the boardroom.

Reason 30: Sleeping with the Boss

Well apparently this might be a reason for why women get into the boardroom...
I've heard several stories from women who have been accused of getting to where they are in organisations because they have obviously slept with either the boss or someone who can influence the boss.

The US based Centre for Work Life Policy found that a staggering 60% of executives and 65% of female executives suspect that salary hikes and plum assignments are being traded for sexual favours.

Interestingly, 15% of women, even at executive level, admitted sleeping with their boss. And 37% of them found it improved their career chances.

A further 34% of executive women in the same survey knew of other women who were sleeping with their boss.

Whilst some women may choose to sleep their way to the top, this is absolutely not true for many, many women. The fact that it's such a strong perception by both men and women is a very big concern.

Reason 31: Sorry Skirts

According to research by the Chartered Institute of Management in 2013, a new phenomenon explains why women aren't getting the top jobs. And it's been given the phrase 'Sorry Skirts.'

Essentially women over-apologise in the workplace, saying sorry much more than their male colleagues.

This is especially true for working mothers. Mums seem to have a natural tendency to over-apologise, over-explain and over-communicate for the choices they make. Whether that's to head off for a drama performance, take a child to the doctors, sports event, the list goes on and on.

Working women lack confidence in their abilities and can often apologise more frequently for what they haven't done, rather than talk about what they have achieved. If they are late for a meeting they will often give all the reasons why. Men on the other hand will pass a simple "Sorry I'm late".

Because this is so inbuilt for us women, we don't tend to be aware of when we are apologising, what triggers us to apologise and how frequently we are doing it. When did you last hear men repeatedly saying sorry. And if you did, what impact do you think that would have?

Reason 32: Office Housework

Boy do I love this phrase. It's from the work of legal scholar Joan Williams. It means the menial, administrative and generally undervalued jobs that need doing in the office.

Examples can include making the coffee; sorting out people's birthdays; organising the Christmas party; invited to and expected to participate in endless committee meetings and taking notes in meetings.

Joan Williams refers to an interview with an ex Harvard lawyer who used the phrase 'mopping up' after her male colleagues.

Sometimes the office housework can have more meaning, but has the double edge sword of no reward or perceived value.

These are often jobs that men don't want to do. Women somehow need to say yes to their bosses (back to that 'Prove it' philosophy) whilst juggling the rest of their stretched workload. These tasks can include managing a mentoring or talent programme.

Or in a recent case a board director client was telling me about – organising a charity ball and then being responsible as well as accountable for ensuring all charities were paid. Whilst these activities are necessary for the organisation and good for branding and employee engagement, do they really enable women to move up the career ladder?

Reason 33: Queen Bee Syndrome

The term Queen Bee Syndrome describes a woman in a position of authority who uses that power to preserve their territory. The term was introduced back in the 1970 by researchers from the University of Michigan.

If you find women are distant from you, unwilling to take your calls, build any kind of working relationship with you or refuse to help you rise through the ranks, then yes, you are experiencing the classic 'Queen Bee' Syndrome.

Queen Bee's chip away at the confidence of younger women or attempt to undermine them (both publically and behind closed doors).
The American Management Association completed a survey in 2011 with 1000 working women. They found that 95% of these women had experienced some form of undermining by another woman.

According to Professor Belle Derks of Leiden University Queen Bee Syndrome may be their response to a 'difficult male environment'. And, here's one of Derk's hypothesis:

"Being a token female executive in a male-dominated environment places women in precarious positions where they have to show that they can play well with the boys rather than mentor the women below them."

In such situations, women take on unwritten rules about how managers behave. For example, lack of socialising after work, no small talk or family talk, micromanaging, behaving as 'in charge' and taking on old-style management behaviour with a focus on the task ahead of the people. Of course, these behaviours lead to alienation and de-motivation.

It's certainly not helping achieve that gender balance.

Reason 34: Men and Traditional Marriages

Well, I found this next report quite shocking. A traditional marriage is one defined as one in which the wife is not employed. Sreedhari Desai, a Harvard Research fellow, was one of three authors of a paper entitled "Marriage Structure and Resistance to Gender Revolution in the Workplace".

Their findings concluded that husbands in these traditional marriages exhibited attitudes, beliefs and behaviours that undermined the role of women in the workplace. In essence, they view women in the workplace through their own marital lens.

In summary, the paper found that these men:
- Viewed the presence of women in the workplace unfavourably
- Perceived that organisations with higher numbers of female employees operated less smoothly
- Perceived organisations with female leaders as relatively unattractive
- Denied qualified female employees opportunities for promotions more frequently

In other words, men look at their marriages as though they are living in the 1950s where women stay at home to look after them and their children.

Perhaps the answer then is not to hire the man with a stay at home wife!

Reason 35: Transgender

There has been a fascinating study by Kristen Schilt examining how 'transgender' men are treated in the workplace. Transgender refers to individuals who change their physical appearance – in this case women who became men.

Within the study Schilt found that men indeed were treated different. She refers to Susan who became Thomas. He was told it had been a good move to fire Susan – due to her incompetence – and now we have a great guy in Thomas.

Another described how he was promoted within two months of doing a job that took a lot longer for women to achieve. A blue-collar worker described how his performance ratings 'sky-rocketed' after his transition despite him doing nothing differently. You can read more of her research in her book: "Just One of the Guys: Transgender Men and the Persistence of Gender Inequality".

Reason 36: Not Playing Golf

Here's a great quote I read online recently:
Women play golf because their careers cannot survive without it.

Harvard Business Review's article "Dysfunction in the Boardroom" found that the percentage of male directors who played golf was twice that of female directors (40% v 20%). Whilst golf reinforces the 'old boys network' it is a place where many decisions and business discussions take place.

HBR research found that many women in the C suite were asked to take up golf. Would you believe that there is actually a company and a website known as "The Grass Ceiling"? Its mission is to:

"use the business of golf as a platform to help level the playing field for women and minorities with their counterparts in the business world."

According to the founder of The Grass Ceiling, Rose Harper, golf is one of the most globally effective tools for networking and deal making.

Another interesting book "Even Par, How Golf Helps Women Gain the Upper Hand in Business" (Leslie Andrews and Adrienne Wax) – found that women are missing out on opportunities to build strong relationships. *"If you can talk about golf, all of a sudden you have a reason to talk to the CEO or your boss two levels above you"*. Out of their research they found 73% of women agreed that playing golf had helped them in business.

Summary of 'Are You For Real?' Reasons:

- Reason 30: Sleeping with the Boss
- Reason 31: Sorry Skirts
- Reason 32: Office Housework
- Reason 33: Queen Bee Syndrome
- Reason 34: Men and Traditional Marriages
- Reason 35: Transgender
- Reason 36: Not Playing Golf

There you have it, 36 reasons why women don't make it to the boardroom! Whilst this might be a frustrating picture, there is a tremendous amount of very practical things we can do. Let's continue.

Part Two

Chapter Seven: Suggested Actions For Organisations

Whilst the focus of this book is what we, as women, can do to improve our chances of boardroom success, it's also important to share some ideas and best practises for what organisations can do too.

This is a short impactful chapter and does not intend to explain how to imbed the suggestions. Instead it provides a list of initiatives that are best practice and should be considered for all organisations interested in gender diversity.

Flexible Working

Back in April 2003 the UK Government introduced legislation called 'The right to request flexible working'. Flexible working has a wide range of opportunities for organisations, including:

- Part time working
- Term time working
- Job sharing
- Compressed hours
- Annual hours
- Working from home
- Mobile working
- Career breaks

Flexible working practises are essential for more senior positions. Too many capable women are leaving due to rigid working patterns and attitudes of 'presenteeism', making it difficult for women to continue to drive their careers forward.

Whilst this is an extremely important strategy, more work needs to be done on embedding greater flexible working for C Suite executives.

For more information on flexible working, check out: http://www.cipd.co.uk

Unconscious Bias Training

Most people, if not everyone in society harbours unconscious views on others. There's an excellent text you can complete online to review what bias you maybe holding. It's called the Implicit Association Test and it was developed by Harvard social psychologist Mahzarin Banaji. Through this testing she has found that the brain naturally places people into groups based upon preconceived stereotypes. Why not take it and find out if you have any bias? (Check out the web-link here: https://implicit.harvard.edu/implicit/)

In another study shared in the Guardian newspaper, 67% of organisations that completed unconscious bias training, found no difference in the number of men v women being hired.

Many organisations are now investing in unconscious bias training for all staff. Google and you'll find a wealth of training companies there to provide help.

Improve Recruitment and Promotion Processes

Other ideas include setting gender targets for managers at every level of promotion. Whilst most women wish to get there on merit, many are being unwittingly discriminated against. By analysing the promotion and recruitment rates this will quickly highlight if and where they may be issues within your organisation. Are there roles or departments where women are less likely to be promoted?

Interestingly, Ernst and Young recently set an internal target of 30% of females and 10% BAME (Black, Asian and Minority Ethnic) representation in new partner intakes.

Another suggestion is to assess and re-think job interview questions. For example, women consistently ask for less salary than men when applying for a new position. Changing the question – "What salary are you looking for?" to "Here's the salary range for this position, where do you think you would be positioned" is a fairer approach.

In November 2015, HSBC has requested 50/50 gender split candidate shortlists from all recruitment agencies. This is becoming a much more common practise.

I've also heard of a number of companies that are now taking names off of CVs to avoid any bias.

Other HR Practices

In addition to recruitment, we know that there are issues in performance reviews, equal pay and enhancing provision for parents. We know from research that there are gender differences in performance reviews (see the report by linguistic Kieran Snyder for Fortune.com). For example the word 'abrasive' was used in many women's performance reviews but never once in a male's performance review.

This would suggest that men need to be much more conscious of focusing on facts and behaviours rather than on personality traits during performance reviews. Having more of a 360 degree feedback culture as part of the performance review process can also be very powerful.
Women can also help the situation by keeping a record of specific achievements and bringing that with them to the performance review.

In terms of equal pay, we know that there is a pay gap between men and women. At the time of writing this is at 20% difference. The answer here is to increase accountability and transparency. Companies must start to review and assess pay levels and scales at all levels. Recently the UK Government has outlined plans to force companies with over 250 staff to reveal the average pay of their male and female employees.

Engaging Men

At a Women International Network (WIN) Conference I attended in Rome, I met a very inspirational speaker - Professor Michael Kimmel who is an American Sociologist at Stony Brook University in New York. He is passionate about gender equality and how we engage men in the debate.

He describes how there are roughly three groups of men:
   a) Those that understand the issue and see the benefits of change
   b) Those that get the issue and 'We will take it from here ladies' approach
   c) The 'Angry White Men' group, those that fear discrimination against them

He rightly believes that we won't get very far in the gender debate without the input of men. He says that gender equality has to be made visible. "Men need to move beyond the idea that a woman 'winning a promotion', 'salary rise' or something else results in a male losing out. He suggests we have to sell the business benefits of diverse teams. He also recommends engaging men in family conversations - after all men are fathers, brothers, and sons too. He also believes that male advocates of the gender equality debate are absolutely key to making change happen.

In addition to the work completed by Michael Kimmel, the global research organisation Catalyst, have also introduced a brand new programme - MARC. MARC stands for Men Advocating Real Change and is a community for men committed to achieving gender equality in the workplace. The website showcases best practices and encourages debates to inspire men who want to expand gender diversity. Take a look at their website: www.onthemarc.org

One other strategy to deploy is in helping men to understand how men and women's thinking is wired. There are differences in how men and women lead, process information and make decisions. There's plenty of research out there. Let's share this and get men to see the value of that difference on a personal and team level.

Sign up for Think Act Report

The UK Government introduced this voluntary campaign - Think Act Report in 2013. The purpose is for organisations to show their commitment to gender diversity. There are several hundred organisations across the UK now participating in this campaign. Show your commitment here: www.gov.uk/think-act-report

Women Leadership Development Programmes

Many companies are choosing to invest in specific women leaders development initiatives. Such programmes can take the form of a six-month cohort of leaders from across the organisation. The cohort attends a range of leadership skills workshops; personal branding; impact and influence, etc. In addition there is often peer coaching and launch events. When you have a look at the Think Act Report initiative you'll find plenty of case studies of such programmes.

You may also consider introducing a women's network, with lunches, speakers, etc.

Join the Women Leaders Association

I'd like to do a plug for an association that I set up in 2015. Its focus is on bringing women from across organisations to:
- Build greater strategic networking across sectors
- Strengthen leadership through 90 day workshops, webinars and audios
- Become respected role models through a programme of mentoring

We have many fabulous, inspiring women who are members.

You can find out more here: www.womenleadersassociation.com

Chapter Eight: Setting Your Compass

We know from our earlier statistics that despite women aspiring to top management positions when they join organisations, many significantly lose that ambition over time. The research from Bain and Co ("Professional women lose confidence, ambition as they reach mid-career") found that it could drop from 43% to only 16%.

One of their findings was that line managers do not appreciate where their female team members are at in terms of their career aspirations.

I've found, through the many years of coaching female leaders, that women are not clear on where they want to go or that they believe their hard work will somehow get them to their magic destination.

As a result, I've identified a simple framework to help women take back control of their career. This approach can provide huge motivation and clarity for both women and their male bosses.

Here are the six steps:

1) Define Your Career Goal

2) Understand Your Value Proposition

3) Build and Leverage a Support Network

4) Get visible

5) Mentors and Career Sponsors

6) Lose the Tiara Syndrome

Step One: Define Your Career Goal

A career goal is a statement that defines where you want to go with your profession using your professional knowledge and expertise. In achieving your career goal, a critical factor is to become recognised as an expert, an authority and a leader within the business.

You must create a detailed description of what you want to accomplish that's a stretch. Ideally it's important to have a time frame on there too (after all, all great goals have time lines on them).

I often see very woolly or vague career goals. "To be great in my job" or "To develop a fab team" or "To enjoy my work every day". This is often followed by "I don't know what I want, my career has just happened to me".

Unless you start to shape what it is that you really want, how on earth are other people going to be able to help you? You will end up in the frustrating middle management ranks with others being promoted ahead of you.

Here are a series of questions I would suggest you start to think about:

- What is the leadership position you would most love to attain? (Take a long-term view. Remember this is not about whether you can do it right now, more a sense of what lights you up).
- What is it about that role that interests you?
- What impact do you want to have in the organisation you are in?
- If you decided to change organisation, what types of organisation would you most like to work for and why?
- What roles do friends of yours have that interest you?
- What is it about those roles that you like?
- Who do you most admire in terms of an inspirational leader? What is it about them / their career that you like?
- What professional growth do you need?
- What are the gaps between where you are now and where you'd like to go?

Next you need to pull together the thoughts into a sentence or concise paragraph.

There is a lot of anecdotal evidence that writing your goal, as if you have already achieved it, seems to achieve faster and strong results. This is much better technique than writing a goal that is based somewhere in the future. One day in the future is typically where it will stay!

Next you need to create a **Career Roadmap**.

Here we break the big vision / career goal statement down into smaller goals. A nice question to ask is "What are the three challenges I need to overcome to achieve this bigger career goal?"

Once you have identified them, you can then break them down into smaller actions with deadlines and rewards.

"I am thrilled that I have recently been offered the role of Director of Marketing. When I look back over the past 5 years, I'm most proud of how I led the strategic review of our product range; volunteered for the organisational change project and found myself a sponsor who provided me with excellent feedback and encouragement."

When coaching my clients, I encourage them to think about their rewards for achieving their career goals and steps along the way. Have some sort of memento / treat / experience that will remind you of how far you have come.

Step Two: Understand Your Value Proposition

A value proposition is usually something that marketeer's write to describe their products, in terms of price, benefits and target market. A Personal Value Proposition is a statement that is at the heart of your personal marketing. It's why are employed. It's the reason you get promoted. It's why others might want you to join their organisations.

In particular, it's creating a statement that feels great when you read it. You should feel a combination of pride and inspiration. A kind of – wow that's me!

Create a strong value proposition is not that difficult…. if you do the right groundwork.

Remember that one of the things women struggle with is in 'self promotion'.

By creating a personal value proposition statement, you are allowing yourself to identify with the things that make you who you are and why you are so valuable.

Here are the elements you need to include in your value proposition:

- Your Leadership Strengths
- Your Business Achievements (Not Your Experience)
- Your Potential

In terms of identifying your **Leadership Strengths**, I would encourage you to first of all complete the Gallup Strengths Finder. Over 14 million people have taken Strengths Finder and it provides your top 5 strengths. It's an excellent tool and is very accurate. There is a small cost to take it. You can find out more here: www.gallupstrengthscenter.com.

Another way of identifying your leadership strengths is to ask others. You can do this simply by taking some time with your team and requesting their feedback. (Be aware that sometimes people can feel a little uncomfortable with feedback in the moment). You can send an email / questionnaire to people you trust. What's important is to understand what it is that you particularly excel at. And you can also complete a 360-feedback exercise. I particularly like the EQi-360 tool, which also includes a review of the strengths of your emotional intelligence too.

Your strengths should describe the qualities and talents you are specifically bringing to the role. It may includes words such as '"Achiever"; "Decisive"; "Warm"; "Professional"; "Collaborative"; "Resilient". What's key is to pull out the 3 – 5 things that best describe your unique qualities.

Next up is to articulate your **Business Achievements.**
Here are some questions to help you think this through:
- What are the things in your career you are most proud of? (Watch that you don't get too fluffy here, e.g. "bringing together a great team"). This next question will help.
- What are things in the business that you have enjoyed doing over the years?
- What difference to the bottom line / to the performance of your team / department / function did these achievements have?
- What do your friends and colleagues say about your achievements?

If you are struggling, see if these prompts help:
- Specific projects you delivered
- Customer satisfaction
- Problem solving
- Recommending a new process that saved time or money
- Improving staff engagement – what did you do?

Once you have identified your business achievement expand on it. Consider the background, problems you faced, what specifically happened, what actions did you take, what were the results and the things that you learnt. This way you will get a great insight into the skills and qualities you are bringing to your roles.

Finally, **identify your Potential.**

I was once asked by a brilliant coach for a metaphor to describe what I wanted to become. The picture that immediately sprang to mind was an oak tree. He asked me what it was about that oak tree that resonated so much with me. I thought about it for a moment and responded that the oak tree represented wisdom and strength. It was a powerful moment for me as I realised that I wanted to share my knowledge with others, to help other people break through the things that were holding them back and to leave some form of legacy. When he asked me what metaphor I used to describe me at the time – my response was "an acorn – small, yet with so much potential within".

This exercise may well work for you. It's a way of tapping into our sub-conscious, which knows exactly what we want and what we are holding onto.

You may also want to find out what potential looks like in your organisation. This is typically the characteristics, skills and abilities that enables others to get on. Once you have a list of the six or seven factors, you can then go and ask your line manager to rate you against them. You will quickly see what the gaps are that you need to focus on.

Once you have your leadership strengths, your business achievements and a clear idea of your potential you can then create your Personal Value Proposition Statement. Here's an example:

"As an experienced Marketing leader, I spearheaded a multi-million pound re-branding exercise. This resulted in a 20% increase in new business. Others described me as resilient; innovative and inspiring throughout the project, which is feedback I'm really proud of. I'm keen to use my languages and move into an international / global role."

Step Three: Build and Leverage a Support Network

Too many women believe that they can achieve their goals and career success through sheer hard work and effort. Many believe they don't have time to get out and about networking and meeting others. Other people don't know how to nurture a strong network that is based upon win-win.

A report by Derek Higgs and Laura Tyson ("The Recruitment and Development of Non Executive Directors", London Business School, 2003) highlighted some fascinating findings:

- Half of the directors they surveyed had been recruited through personal friends and contacts
- Only 4% had a formal interview
- Only 1% obtained the role through an advertisement.

EY (Ernst and Young) recently commissioned research to look into how professionals are networking now and how this may change in the future.

Here are some of their findings:

- Networking is now seen as a "Core Business Skill"
- Apparently 1 in 4 professionals DON'T network at all
- And 65% of people prefer to network in person

I love this definition of networking by Angela Hackett:

"Networking is talking and connecting with people with NO ulterior motive. It's a desire to learn and expand your world."

Networking is about relationships. Women are naturally great at building relationships. In fact, networking should be very comfortable for women and seen as an essential part of your role. It should have as high a priority as your daily shower or morning cup of coffee.

Review the Strength of Your Current Network
- Who is in your network?
- Think about your network in terms of operational, personal and strategic
- How strong is your network? Give the names a rating out of 10.
- How well does your network know what you want?
- How well do you know what your network members want?
- And how often are you serving people in your network? How often do you meet?

Building Relationships
Once you've reviewed the strength and depth of your network, the next step is to think about what you are going to do to build the relationship.

Women are natural collaborators and most instinctively want to help others.
Here are a few ideas of the things you can give when you are considering networking:
- Your time
- Access to your contacts and resources
- Your expertise
- Opportunities you are aware of
- Recommendations
- Networking events / learning resources that maybe of value
- Tips and insights

Create an Action Plan
I'd recommend you pick three key people initially. Come up with a 3 – 6 month action plan of how you can strengthen that relationship.

Developing a strong powerbase puts you in a position of strength and will very quickly improve your visibility.

Next you must get a mentor and a potential sponsor.

Step Four: Mentors & Career Sponsors

Mentors play a really important role in the development and retention of women leaders. One piece of research* found that 95% of all women had never sought a mentor at work. This is staggering. Another survey found that 1 in 5 women had never had a mentor. *Women leaders who do have a mentor have performed better, achieved a higher salary and achieved more promotions.*

Here are my top tips for seeking a mentor:

- *Decide on why you want a mentor and what benefit they will bring.* For example, do you want a mentor as a sounding board? Would you like to speak with someone who has broken through the barriers you are experiencing? Do you want specific advice with situations you are faced with?
- *What would be in it for the mentor?* Consider why the mentor would want to mentor you. Are you reliable? Are you going to implement advice and feedback? Will you ensure it feels a great use of his / her time?
- *Use your network to find a great mentor.* Think about whom you know / whom do they know? Does anyone in the organisation inspire you? Think about off-line activities too, e.g. your Linked-In network.
- *Make sure there is a good fit.* This is the tricky part. You need to ensure that it 'feels' right. Is there a mutual respect? Is there genuine warmth from both parties? Does it feel as though you are being listened to?
- *Keep the relationship 'healthy'.* Make sure you have a fixed time for your discussions. Decide how frequently and a suitable venue. Ensure that you can be open and honest with each other about how it's going and build in time to review.

Career Sponsors

A career sponsor is someone who is prepared to put his or her neck on line for you.
- These are individuals who value what you do; your skills; your attitude and your results.
- They will support and advise you.
- They will recommend you to potential projects and positions.
- In essence they are 'willing to go out and bat for you'.

Reading "The Sponsor Effect: Breaking Through the Last Glass Ceiling (Harvard Business Review Research Report", December 2010) I was shocked to read the following:

While men in general are 25 percent more likely than women to have a sponsor, senior level men are 50 percent more likely.

What are the Benefits of a Sponsor?

There are many:

- Introducing you to people of influence
- Advice you on high stake meetings
- Providing you with high visibility assignments
- Making connections for you
- Giving you critical feedback on skills gaps
- Propelling you to the list of potential candidates
- And on and on the list goes

Ideally a sponsor should be two to three levels ahead of you. Find someone enough to make a difference and still be close enough to stay in touch.

Finding a Sponsor

Don't expect to walk up to someone and ask him or her to be a sponsor. There are a number of unwritten rules.
- Firstly it takes time and effort.
- Secondly, your sponsor needs to trust you, believe in you, see that you have credibility and will not let them down.

The best sponsors are always on the lookout for potential talent, so you have to find ways to get yourself noticed. Here are a few ideas:

- Volunteer for high visibility assignments
- Consider the strength of your current relationships – who do you know and who knows you
- Join professional networks
- Attend industry and corporate events

If there is someone you would love to have as a career sponsor, you need to plan out how you want to best work with him or her. Explain how you are keen to progress and ask if they would be willing to help. What did they do to get on in their careers? How would they advise you to go about achieving your career goals?
Then ask how you can help them. Are there any projects you can help or support with? Are there ways you can bring your talents and expertise to their work?

Finding a sponsor is THE best way to achieve a place in the boardroom. You have to find a suitable sponsor and work hard at maintaining and growing the relationship. Don't be mistaken that you will achieve it by yourself. It won't happen.

Step Five: Get Visible

Creating a network is only one part of the agenda. The next step is to create specific strategies to get yourself visible. This is such an important strategy.

Here's a way of thinking about your network and about how you can get visible. It's based upon a wonderful article by Harvard Business Review, "How Leaders Create and Use Networks" by Herminia Ibarra and Mark Hunter.

There are three different networks that we need to be actively managing.

Operational Network
The most common network is an operational network, i.e. the men and women we work with to get our day-to-day objectives and projects delivered. This is where most women spend their time.

There are two other networks that we also have to focus on:

Personal Network
The personal network is about networking to help strengthen our knowledge, our leadership strengths, our qualities, etc. Examples include professional associations, alumni groups, leaders in their field, mentors, and referrals. You can offer to work on an organising committee, to write articles or speak at local events.

Strategic Network
The strategic network is one that may be referred to as the political navigation of the corporate world. A successful strategic network is all about leverage, lobbying and influencing others. It's about figuring out future priorities and challenges for the organisation. It's working with key stakeholders.

Use the questions above to consider how you can increase your three networks with the filter. For example, what can I give in exchange for raising my visibility?

Step Six: Get Rid of Tiara Syndrome Thinking

In the earlier part of this book we referred to the issue of the Tiara Syndrome. Too many women keep their head down and genuinely believe that their achievements will speak for themselves. When we first start out in our careers, this is a critical route for getting noticed. Because when we hit our mid career and certainly into senior leadership this is simply a given, you need some extra ingredients to get promoted.

Too many women fall into the 'loyalty trap' – my hard work will enable me to get the success I long for. I know of so many women who are waiting to break through the glass ceiling, desperate to get that recognition and to land a position on the board. They take on more and more workload. They deliver over and above what is expected. Delivery is their absolute focus.

This thinking has to go!

Career success is not about the volume of work you deliver.

Instead you have to lift your head up. You have to get involved in projects outside of your area of responsibility. You have to align your work to the strategic objectives of the business. You have to talk about how the work you are doing is making a difference to the business. You have to stand back and rethink how you are interacting with those around you. Otherwise you will be stuck forever, wondering what else you have to deliver to prove your capability.

By setting a clear compass and following these steps, you will be well on your way to taking control of your career. You will be able to get noticed and get visible. You will be demonstrating your value add and talking the language of success.

Chapter Nine: Building Your Inner Confidence

Despite how successful on the outside many women leaders appear to be, I find in my professional experience, time and time again that these women have a real issue with inner confidence. This might be in the form of feeling "not good enough" or "I'll get found out" or "I don't particularly like myself" or a never ending inner critic that seems to metaphorically beat us up throughout the day.

As we saw earlier in the book, our confidence is often to do with our conditioning. This includes the influence of parents and other respected elders; the environment we were brought up in; and the reaction of peers and others to our beliefs and behaviour.

More importantly, what can we do about it?

In this chapter I'd like to share a range of techniques and tools you can use to build your inner confidence.

I am Enough

This is an extremely powerful yet very simple technique. Firstly let me credit this to the inspirational woman who implemented this approach. Her name is Marisa Peer and she is an international therapist and incredible woman. She's written books on confidence and losing weight. She is one of the most loved speakers of Mindvalley.

This 'trick of the mind' is quite simply to repeat over and over again: "I am enough'. Marisa describes it as a simple daily habit to change your life. I absolutely believe this to be true. Not only has it led to incredible shifts in my life but also it absolutely has in the life of my clients.

Why is this so powerful? Well according to Marisa, many of us over eat, drink excessively, and are compulsive shoppers, over indulgent cleaners and on and on it goes. The reason? We have an inner emptiness of not feeling enough.

The lovely thing about this phrase is that we don't have to prove anything to anyone. We simply learn to fall back in love with who we are and the gifts we have. All we need to do is repeat the words "I am enough" over and over again.

I take this a step further with my clients and get them to place the words onto post it notes and plaster everywhere! On mirrors in the bathroom; on their kettle; phone; PC; dashboard – anywhere that they visit throughout the day. Whilst it seems a little odd (and you may need to warn your family) the subconscious is constantly reading the message over and over again. Your conscious mind will soon forget the stickies are there. Try it. You may be amazed at how this simple process transforms your life.

By the way, you can find out more about Marisa at her website: www.marisapeer.com.

Inner Talk

Let's talk a bit more broadly about the power of our inner mind. Most of us know that we tend to silently talk to ourselves in our head. You may be rehearsing a meeting that you have coming up or reminding yourself of a shopping list.

You may not know that in the 1990s, neuroscientists found that part of our brain mechanisms are active during inner talk as well as when we speak out loud.

Unfortunately for most of us, the mind has developed a rich pattern of inner talk that is constantly demanding, comparing and judging. Perhaps more surprisingly is that this inner talk is there to protect us. It's there to keep us safe.

I read a lovely example of this on the website www.pathwaytohappiness.com. They referenced a time when our memories and our logic are being formed. When we are very small we are allowed to be in the moment with no boundaries as to what's possible.

Imagine playing outside one day and seeing a dog. Our instinct would be to go and play with the dog. Now imagine that dog unfortunately bites us. Our memory stores this experience. Next time we see a dog, there's a protective inner voice that says: 'Whoa, there's a dog, watch out in case you get bitten'.

Whilst this is a small example it gives you an idea of how our experiences can shape our beliefs and our thought processes. Over the years we build billions of dendrites or neurons pathways in the brain. The more we think the same thoughts, the bigger and thicker and faster these dendrites become.

My belief is that we allow our inner talk to take over the running of our lives. We allow ourselves to fear failure; to fear criticism; to fear rejection, etc.

The good news is that we can break the pattern.

Gremlin Magic

Another wonderful book by Rick Carson, called "Taming Your Gremlin". That's his great way of describing the 'narrator in your head'. Here's a part of his definition of the gremlin:

"He accompanies you throughout your life. He's with you when you wake and when you go to sleep. He wants you to accept his interpretation of reality."

Our gremlins are typically at the core of our worries and our fears.

Here are a few things you can do to quiet the hold our gremlins have on us:

- Shine the spotlight on them.
- Give the gremlin a name
- Change the voice – make it faster, slower, deeper, higher, change it's gender
- Draw them
- Say thanks!

Eventually your gremlin will shrivel up! It's a fun practise.

Positive Affirmations

In much the same was as I described the 'I am enough' process above, affirmations are a brilliant way to help build positive thoughts.

Brian Tracy is a world-renowned speaker and author of personal development. He believes that 95% of our emotions are determined "by the way we talk to ourselves". He likens our minds to that of a garden and emphasises that weeds will quickly grow if we don't take deliberate care.

Affirmations are a daily practice of positive thinking. Essentially we repeat phrases over and over again that help us to feel good about ourselves. These phrases are positive statements that describe a desired state. Here are some wonderful affirmations from Louise Hay (another wonderful inspirational guru in the field of self development):

- "I choose to feel good about myself every day. Every morning I remind myself that I can make the choice to feel good. This is a new habit for me to cultivate."
- "Peace begins with me. The more peaceful I am inside, the more peace I have to share with others. World peace really does begin with me."

- "Today is going to be a really, really good day!"
- "I am patient, tolerant and diplomatic".
- "Every experience I have is perfect for my growth".

There are millions of affirmations you can download on the web. The trick is to find ones that resonate with you and keep reading them. Have them on your phone, so if you are early for a meeting you can have a quick read of them.

I'd really encourage you to start this practise – you'll be amazed at how good you start to feel about yourself.

Gratitudes

Here's another wonderful practice. And it's one I found in a wonderful book called: "The Magic" by Rhonda Byrne. There is even scientific research that an attitude of gratitude is a good health choice. (See the work of the Greater Good Science Centre at the University of California, Berkeley for examples of initiatives). Dr Robert Emmons has eight years of intensive research on the topic shared in his book: "Thanks! How the New Science of Gratitude Can Make You Happier".

By focusing on the positives in life, will put you in a better frame of mind and help you with your sense of worth and your self-esteem.

This practice requires you to write between 5 and 10 things every day you are grateful for. These don't have to be big things. They can be as simple as a cup of coffee you enjoyed or a beautiful sunset. They might include conversations you had with people or a book you read. What's great about this process (if you stick to it) is that you will start to actively look for more and more good things throughout your day!

I promise you that the suggestions above work! It's about discipline and focus.

Belief Shift

And yet, sometimes, I have found that my clients need deeper work to shift beliefs that have been with them and held them back for years. There are a number of processes I use that can really help to shift these beliefs once and for all. The downside is that they tend to need someone to help you work through them.

I've been pondering on this for a while. How can I help people who want to work on belief changes on their own? To my delight, I came across a wonderful process by Morty Lefkoe. It's a free resource and it's a great practise. Here's the link: http://recreateyourlife.com/free

There are two other wonderful resources I would recommend. One is the book: "You can Heal Your Life" by Louise Hay. The other is "The Journey" by Brandon Bay. Both of these are focused on removing emotional issues that we are stuck with. I've worked with both and found them to be extremely useful.

Positive Visualisation

The next process – that of positive visualisation is one of my favourites. This is the process of creating a picture of the goals you want to achieve. The power of the picture is that it activates our subconscious minds to being bringing that picture towards us.

Athletes have been using this process since the 1960s. Essentially what you do is to create a movie in your mind of the goals you want to create. You need to add as much detail as possible. This should include noise, colour, feelings and movement.

Above all feel grateful for what you want to create in your life and let it go. That means to let go of the outcome. Don't demand it to happen or worry about it happening. Believe it will come.

If you do this practise everyday (and I spend only a few minutes every morning) you genuinely will feel better and more focused about yourself.

Positive Mental Food

I love this idea – 'positive mental food'. It's another one of Brian Tracy's excellent phrases. Essentially it's about feeding you mind with uplifting information and ideas. Things that make you feel more confident about yourself and your world.

Here are some ideas:
- Stop watching the news! By all means download an app and have a quick look at the headlines. But the news is full of such doom and gloom that we end up feeding our gremlins.
- Read inspirational books, magazines and articles.
- Read "Acres of Diamonds" for an excellent story for how we should focus on what's around us rather than believing our dreams our somewhere else.

Here's a list of positive uplifting films (I love them!):
- The Bucket List
- It's a Wonderful Life
- The Pursuit of Happiness
- Pay it Forward
- Shackleton
- Yes Man

Fake it 'til You Make It

I couldn't close this chapter without making reference to Amy Cuddy and her TedGlobal 2012 talk. Cuddy believes (and it worked for her) that if we assume a power pose for just two minutes it will change your life! The focus here is on body language. Amy Cuddy (who is a social psychologist) found that our body language also shapes who we are and how we feel about ourselves.

Essentially by standing tall and proud, even if we don't feel confident – has a positive effect on how we feel about ourselves. Try it!

These strategies are all designed to build your inner confidence. There are no quick wins. But the more of them you can do, the quicker the turnaround will be.

As Brian Tracy once said:

"Mental fitness is like physical fitness. Your self esteem will develop with training and practise."

I have recommended these approaches and seen enormous changes in my clients. These are clients working in the boardroom and those looking to break through the glass ceiling.

I promise you that if you deploy these techniques in conjunction with other recommendations, you will achieve your career aspirations and see your life transform!

Chapter Ten: Becoming a Courageous Leader

Advancing professionally is about stepping out of your shadow and shifting the 'head down and prove it' philosophy too many women have. It takes much more than technical expertise to get ahead. Don't get me wrong; having a proven track record is really important for women. You have to have a clear area of expertise before you can get noticed.

Having courage is about seizing opportunities, being tenacious, speaking the 'language of power', being ambitious and having that strong inner confidence to truly believe in your potential. What would your life and career look like if you had unlimited courage?

Courageous leadership is needed no matter what your level you are at in your organisation.

In my experience, there are three foundations for women who wish to demonstrate and be known for their courageous leadership:

Ambition: thinking big; leading from the heart and inspiring strong followership

Voice: calling things out; influencing and communicating powerfully

Business Acumen: knowing where the organisation is going, understanding strategic and financial targets.

Courageous Ambition.

Let's start with ambition. I was recently talking to an ex retail CEO who said that whilst he would love to fill his boardroom with more women: "Where are they?"
I was somewhat taken aback by his question, as there are so many women I know and work with who have a high amount of ambition. He feels strongly that the women just aren't visible.

Interestingly we know from research that many women when they join organisations have a lot of ambition.

So, what can women do?

Here are a number of ideas.

Career Ambition

Firstly women can and must consider what they want to achieve in their career. It's very easy to let the limiting beliefs creep in: "What me?"

Imagine if you had no limitations on what you could be, do or have in your career. Imagine that you had the experience, the education and the contacts you ever needed. Imagine you could not fail.

What would you do? Who would you become as a leader? Start dreaming big. And start writing it down. (We share more of this thinking in the chapter on your True North.)

Once you have a strong sense of what's important to you and where you are heading, you need to share it. You need to get visible; seek feedback and ensure others know of your passions and your ambitions.

Leadership Dashboard

My wonderful coach trainer, Andrew Neitlich (founder of the Centre for Executive Coaching), introduced me to a fabulous tool known as a Leadership Dashboard. This is an excellent framework for not only structuring your thinking, but also for getting your thinking down on paper. It's a tool you can carry with you and keep your decision making in alignment with the things that matter.

Within the dashboard, you can include: your vision; your strengths; your key objectives; your personal development goals and the people who are going to help you achieve your ambitions.

Leadership v Management

There's a trap many leaders (both men and women) fall into. That's the trap of becoming a busy manager. We often believe that the bigger our 'to do' list; the more emails we have and working extraordinary long hours will of course prove our worth.

Unfortunately the world needs more leaders not more managers. True leadership is leading from the heart. It's leading with a purpose, leading for the things you care about. It's dealing with the unknown; it's listening and trusting your instinct; it's making decisions without having all the facts and answers.

We have to take a regular step back from the busyness of our lives. You will never be able to get on top of everything within your to do list. Adopt the 80/20 rule and build in time for planning and reflection. At least once a month take time out to reflect on where you are heading and the progress you are making.

Followership

Courageous leaders always create strong followership. As a leader, it's critical to create the right culture, understanding and ways of working that will enable your team to thrive. It's about letting go of the detail and trusting someone else to mess up; to do things differently to you and perhaps to even outshine you.

Another CEO I heard speak recently shared how she had filled her team with people far better at their jobs than she could ever be. It's helped her transform the organisation and transform her leadership. She's had to let go. She doesn't have the technical knowledge to interfere. But what she does do is set very clear expectations.

Creating Strong Engagement

Engagement is a bit of a buzzword at the moment. And it's no surprise when you see the high levels of stress that exist in our workplace. If you'd like to build stronger engagement with your team, then remember that small informal conversations about performance go a long way – especially when they include teachable moments about different situations and details. It's important to prepare for interactions with others, and here are some powerful questions you might like to consider:

- What do I expect from you? How clearly can I articulate my expectations? What's my message to you if these expectations are not met?
- What are you doing well? What are your particular strengths?
- What, if anything, can you be doing better?
- What, if anything, do I want you to do better?
- How can I help?

While all of these questions are important, the last question is especially important. It shows the employee that the leader cares, and is not merely abdicating responsibility or shifting blame.

I remember once a CEO asking his direct reports the following question:

> *"How can I be the best boss you have ever had?"*

He didn't ask this only once; he asked it again and again.

Courageous Voice

Women in particular need to be stronger at getting heard. Sheryl Sandberg in her excellent book, talks about women needing to 'Lean In'. To me, having a courageous voice means a number of things:

- Being brave in meetings where you feel uncomfortable (whether that's a seniority thing or a lack of knowledge)
- Calling things out in the moment
- Become an expert influencer
- Communicating powerfully
- Saying no

Let's look at these in a little more depth.

Being Brave in Meetings

When we sit back and listen without contributing we are giving out strong signals that we don't have a lot to say. Sometimes we don't have the answers or the solutions. But many times we can ask questions for clarity that will have just as much impact.

In the excellent book 'Courageous Intelligence' by Judith Glasers, she refers to the nature of different conversations.

- Level 1 conversations are those that are 'transactional' in nature.
- Level 2 conversations focus on influence and power.
- Level 3 conversations are those that are transformational in nature. They are the ones that occur without judgement, without answer, when we offer to co-create a solution. It's about sharing insights and asking curious questions.

So if you notice you are sitting back in meetings or teleconferences, ask yourself this:

- What question can I ask to seek clarity, move this conversation forward or create insight?

Calling Things in the Moment

There's a very influential, authentic leader I know who is simply brilliant at calling things in the moment. She has a gift of being able to read a room; sense the energy and notice her own emotional reaction to what is going on. Over time she has bravely listened to her intuition and shared what she is noticing.

She'll ask, in a lovely, non-threatening way: "I notice that you seem uncomfortable with that decision. What's concerning you right now?" I can't tell you how powerful this strategy is. Try it and see.

Expert Influencer

Many years ago Sheppard Moscow introduced me to a wonderful influencing model. It's based upon the concept of Push & Pull influencing. A push style of influence is one in which your agenda is more important than the other person.

Let's say you want the board to take a specific course of action. Here you would typically present lots of facts, figures and reasons as to your suggestion is the best one. You may choose to increase the impact of your message by adding some rewards or outlining risks if that approach is not taken.

On the other hand, a pull style of influence is one in which you seek to find out where the other person is coming from. You ask questions about what is important to them, you listen, you summarise.

There are a number of other suggestions you should look to master too:

- Compelling stories
- Metaphor and symbols
- Visioning the future

Communicating Powerfully

The Power of Three

People remember 'threes'. Every great book, film and presentation has a beginning, middle and an end. The key is to identify three messages you want to get across. Once you've achieved that, you can add three facts or ideas to back up your points. It's a very powerful technique that can truly transform your communication impact.

Language Strategies

Earlier in this book we discussed how the language patterns of women are one of the inhibitors to success. Here are a few practical things you can do to increase your impact:

- Drop the hedges, e.g. I think; basically; apparently; I just; I'm not really sure
- Stop raising your voice at the end of a sentence
- Stop using 'tags', i.e. okay? Don't you think? Isn't it?

Body Language

As well as our language patterns, you must master your body language too. Here's some NOT to dos:

- Look away when stating something important - keep the eye contact at all times
- Scurry into a room - walk with confidence
- Leave a meeting and dash off to the next one - build in time to talk to your colleagues
- Tilt you head - how often do you see men tilting their head when listening?

One final top tip I'd like to share is to encourage you to watch Amy Cuddy's Tedx presentation entitled: 'Fake It Till You Make It'. An excellent confidence video.

Saying No

Women leaders often struggle with saying no to others. Why? Well as we saw earlier we have early conditioning (about how we should behave) and expectations around proving ourselves.

What can happen is that women end up in overwhelm and taking on more than they can physically handle.

This typically means working longer and longer hours; eating into evenings and weekends; productivity being affected and 'me time' being well and truly squished. In addition, women find they have no time to get involved in other initiatives; networking or increasing their visibility.

Therefore, women have to be better at saying no. And here are a few suggestions for how to do it:

Explain the consequences of the request

- Talk about how this will impact on other work in your day; request additional resource or ask what you can let go of to deliver this as well.

Set boundaries from the start

- If you have agreed you'll work from home once a week, stick to it. Make sure you and your boss are aligned about how you work, how decisions are made, updates shared and issues logged. Flag this as a potential issue up front and request guidance for what to do.

Throw in some alternatives

- Rather than a straight forward no, throw in some options that may not have been considered

The 'Reasoned' No

- Say no and give your reason for it: "here's why I can't"

The 'Sleeping' No

- Simply. "I'll let you know tomorrow when I've had time to think"

It's a fine line for women to maintain their authenticity whilst becoming 'assertive'. *Don't confuse aggression for assertiveness.*

Demonstrating Business Acumen

There is an excellent TedX video by Susan Colantuono entitled "The Missing 33%". It's a terrific insight into one of the reasons women are not getting promoted. She believes that successful leadership is made up of three parts:

- Personal Impact
- Leadership
- Business Skills

Through her research she found that Business Acumen is a 'given', i.e. it is expected that executives have a grasp of the business; the strategic objectives and the financial levers. When investigating this further, she found that the majority of men are given feedback and development opportunities to enhance their business skills compared to few women.

Business acumen has twice as much weighting as other leadership skills. Women therefore must develop their knowledge and more importantly become more visible.

Demonstrating Business Understanding

It's important to have conversations about the business and to be asking questions about business performance. Dan Kennedy in his book "No BS Time Management for Entrepreneurs" provides an excellent business framework, which I believe, is just as applicable for corporate leaders.

He suggests you answer the following questions at least once a week to keep you ahead of the game.

What do you know that you didn't know last week?

- About your company
- A key competitor
- Your company customers
- Economic trends that may affect your organisation
- Your profession
- A news item that may impact your organisation
- Ideas for productivity improvement

Next, I'd encourage you to plan how you can build your visibility around these topics. Who can you share and debate these topics with?

Financial Awareness

It's critical for all women leaders who wish to get a seat at the board to be able to:

- Read and understand an income statement
- Read and understand a balance sheet
- Understand cash flow statements
- Know the difference between cash and profitability for your company
- Understand the ratio of return on assets
- Get clear on the key drivers and the variable costs

Finance is at the heart of any business. It's not just the numbers you need to know but being able to ask the 'what, why and how' to inform decisions. How does your company make money? Sustain profits?

To help broaden your financial awareness, I'd like to do a plug for a very dear friend of mine – Andi Lonnen. Andi is an ex finance director who has set up www.financetrainingacademy.com. Please check it out.

Strategic Thinking

The third area to develop is your strategic thinking. There are many excellent and practical tools to help you develop. One of my favourites is the Strategic Dashboard. This is a one-page summary of all of the key drivers in the business and a snapshot in time as to what's important.

- Your Business Vision and Mission (why does your organisation exist)
- Your Values (and the way you do business)
- You Customer - not just who they are but also:
    o Potential for future growth
    o Life cycle
    o Share of the market
    o Buying criteria
    o Opportunities to serve them better
- Product range and profitability

- Competitors and their key niche

- Environmental factors such as government, society, technology

- Performance measures

If you've not already done this, I'd recommend you regularly do a strategic review with your business / team / function. Working through these suggestions to sharpen your business thinking and improve your visibility and your impact.

In summary, this chapter is quite a hefty one! There are many different aspects to courageous leadership and so many ways women can increase their impact in the business. I've looked to simplify it into three separate headers:

- Have Ambition

- Have a Voice

- Demonstrate Your Business Acumen

Identify your hot spots and your development areas. Hopefully you have a significant number of approaches at your disposal. You don't have to use them all! They are designed to increase your flexibility. Think of them as a toolbox – you need different approaches depending on what the problem is.

Chapter Eleven: True North Leadership

I've introduced this chapter because many of the women leaders I have coached come to me with a common frustration. They've outwardly achieved a lot. Perhaps it's a boardroom role; an international assignment; a healthy salary; big budget or opportunities to grow the business.

And yet, these women on the inside feel frustrated. *They know there is something more to their lives. They know what they are doing now isn't it. They want greater fulfilment, meaning, hope and inspiration.*

As a result I introduced a coaching programme that supports women to get clear on their 'True North' and their purpose in life.

The programme follows a 7-step framework:

1. Life's Journey
2. Legacy and Purpose
3. Leadership Impact
4. Values and Motivations
5. Integrating Life Roles
6. Daily Practices
7. Support Network

Step One: Life Journey

One of the most powerful techniques for gaining insight and perspective on your leadership is to map your life's journey. This is a visual exercise so you'll need to get a large sheet of paper and pens. Divide the paper with a straight line across the middle. Draw a vertical line on the life of the page. Above the line represents happy moments in your life and below the line represents low moments in your life.

Chart your life in terms of events from a specific age. You may choose your early childhood, early teens or perhaps when you left home. Consider your life in 'chunks of time', e.g. every 5 years. Record the things that happened.

Next consider how these events have shaped you as a leader. What specifically influenced the choices you have made? Who has had a big impact on your life? How have you changed and grown?

In the wonderful book by Bill George "Finding Your True North"; he encourages leaders to also consider their 'crucible'. A crucible is "an experience that tests leaders to the limits." Examples include losing a job; critical feedback; getting divorced; death of a loved one.

A crucible moment typically tests you to re-evaluate who you are; what's important to you; your values and your view on the world. Take some time now to consider your crucible moments in life. What happened? How have these events changed you? What have been your learnings and insights?

Step Two: Legacy and Purpose

Next we need to spend time reflecting about your legacy and your purpose. I believe it is our life's journey to discover our true purpose but the path to get there is full of learnings and insights. Fortunately there are things we can do to speed up the process.

The questions that follow are easy to read and certainly difficult to answer. I know as I find them difficult too! Get yourself a lovely journal and take your time thinking them through.

Passions

- What are the things you like to talk about?
- What do you like to do in your spare time? (These are not chores)
- What do you enjoy reading?
- What films and TV programmes do you enjoy watching?
- What would your ideal weekend be?
- When you were a child, what did you dream about doing?
- And as a teenager?
- What were some of your favourite pastimes?
- If money and time were no obstacles, what would you do?
- If you won the lottery, what would you do? (Assuming you already did the big spending spree!).

In Flow

- Where do you lose all sense of time?
- What are you doing in the moments when you feel at peace / happy / content with the world?
- What do others thank you for?
- What activities give you energy? Conversely, what things take your energy away?
- At work, when do you feel at your best?

Legacy

- What are the higher reasons (beyond pay and rewards) that bring you to work each day?
- What did (do) your parents / partner / key influencers say about your skills and talents?
- What are the things you are proud of achieving so far in your life?
- If you had to guess what your calling was, what would you say? (Don't worry about how silly it might sound, how impractical or how distant it feels, go with your gut).

And finally, here's a lovely question I first heard from the inspirational Steve Radcliffe (author of Future Engage Deliver):

- What is the future organisation you would be proud to help build?

Step Three: Leadership Impact

Perhaps one of the most powerful things you can do to get a sense of your leadership purpose and impact is to ask other people.

We can so often operate in a bubble. We hope and pray that we are having the right impact and inspiring others.

But how often do we really know. Too often we shy away from hearing the truth. If you want to grow as a leader and find your True North, you really must be brave and ask for feedback.

The first step is to reflect on the following questions:

- What's the impact you think you are having on others?
- Where might you be inspiring others right now?
- Where might you be 'casting a shadow'?
- Who is the leader you most want to be?
- What might others 'feel' when they are around you?
- What's the impact when you are not at your best?

Select a cross section of people who you know, e.g. your boss, peers, team, suppliers, family, friends, etc.

Next select two or three questions you'd most like to get feedback on. Ideally see if you can enlist the support of a friend, mentor or coach.

Once you receive the feedback, it's important to act on it. Create an action plan with specific goals that you feel you can work on and achieve.

Step Four: Values and Motivations

Successful leaders are crystal clear on their values and motivations. You won't feel inspired if you are working in an environment that does not deliver to your values.

When you get clear on your values, you'll find they provide a compass for your decision-making. What I've noticed about defining values is that often clients pick the values they 'should' have, e.g. family; health; security. Now, of course, these are important, but your true values are present in all of your interactions with others.

Remember that as a leader others are watching you. You are setting the tone and the culture for 'how you want it to be around here'. Here are a few examples:

- Achievement
- Integrity
- Challenge
- Variety
- Happiness
- Fun
- Creativity

(There are many more - in fact I have a sheet with over 400 potential values!)

Once you have identified your values, I recommend to my clients that they also define what their values mean to them. E.g. How are you building in fun into your every day leadership? What does it look like in practical terms?

Alongside our values it's also important to identify our external motivations. These are typically more 'ego' driven factors that I've found many women struggle to articulate. Another way of defining our motivations is the ways in which we like to be recognised, both within your organisation and with family / friends.

Here are a few examples of extrinsic motivations.

- Money
- Position / role
- Brand association
- Feedback
- Competition
- Personal Development
- Travel

I've seen many women become trapped with the trimmings of success. This is not to say that these factors are not important. In fact it's the opposite. We must identify with the things that do give us 'proud' moments.

Write a list of the things that make you feel proud of whom you are. What are the 'external recognition' factors that motivate you?

The key is to achieve a healthy balance between our values that drive us and the motivations that reward us.

Step Five: Integrating Life Roles

Another reason we can feel 'trapped' in a successful job is because we are not balancing and integrating our different life roles.

Consider for a moment the many different hats you have to wear. For example:

- Family roles: Mother, daughter, sister, wife, etc.
- Career roles: Boss, peer, team member, etc.
- Community involvement
- Managing the home
- Balancing health and well-being
- Personal development

A simple exercise is to assess how satisfied you are right now with each aspect of your life.

Next is to stand back and consider what happiness truly looks like for each of the roles.

It's not easy to achieve happiness in every aspect, so next is to prioritise.

Here are a few more questions to help you think through your priorities:

- What aspects of your life do you need to put greater focus on?
- What would your 'reason' why be for each area?
- Are your 'why's compelling enough?
- How does each life role align with your career and professional life?
- What actions and changes do you need to make?

Step Six: Daily Practises

Over the past decade, I've been very interested in understanding what stand out leaders do with their time. We all have the same time on the planet. And I certainly want to make the most use of my time!

I also believe that leaders who wish to discover their true north have to nourish their spirit energy. There are many daily practises you can put in place to 'nourish your soul'. Here are a few of my favourites.

Meditation

By focusing a few minutes every day you can experience many benefits:
- Happiness
- Better sleep
- Appreciative of life
- Reducing stress
- Improving brain function

There are many different types of meditation: guided meditation (where someone talks the whole way through); mantra meditations (where you repeat words and sounds) and breathing meditations where you focus on your breath.

Try all different approaches to see what works for you the best. Don't be too hard on yourself. It will take practise and effort. If you'd like to explore this further, check out one of my favourite websites: www.chopracentermeditation.com.

Gratitudes

Gratitude can quite literally change your life. Recent research has shown that regularly writing about the things we are grateful for can significantly increase our well-being and our life satisfaction. There's a wonderful book called 'The Magic' by Rhonda Byrne (author of The Secret). Here's an adaptation of what she says to do when practising gratitude.

Every day make a note of 10 things you are grateful for during the day. What were the moments that made your heart sing / that inspired you / that shifted your perspective? Be as specific as you can and *feel* the thanks and gratitude as you write and reflect.

Visioning

Spend time each day focusing on the future you. What do you want to create? Build upon the legacy questions from earlier and create mental movies in your mind. By playing these over and over, you begin to build new mental neurons.

As the wonderful writer Napoleon Hill once said:
"Whatever the mind can conceive and believe, it can achieve."

Step Seven: On-going Support

No personal development book would be complete without a look at how you can continue to grow as a leader. As you can tell, True North Leadership is much more introspective. It requires us to tap into our 'spirit energy' as a leader - the things that *inspire* us to move forwards.

I truthfully and whole-heartedly believe you cannot do this on your own. My business took off once I invested in my development.

The first step is to create a Leadership Development Plan. You can include your vision, purpose, legacy, values, motivations and your life priorities. Use it as a guide or a compass to navigate your career decisions.

Next make sure you have a network of like-minded professionals. Individuals who can challenge you and keep you on track.

Finally, I'd advise you to invest in a coach. A coach will help you get there far quicker than if you attempt to do this on your own. A coach will hold you accountable and believe in your potential so much more than you ever will be yourself.

For more information on coaching programmes, please visit:

www.handbagsintheboardroom.com

Printed in Great Britain
by Amazon